Res Gestae
Things Done

Naida Haxton AM

Published by:
Boolarong Press
655 Toohey Road
Salisbury Qld 4107
Australia
www.boolarongpress.com.au

National Library of Australia Cataloguing-in-Publication entry:
Creator: Haxton, Naida J. author.
Title: Res gestae : things done / Naida Haxton.
ISBN: 9781925522051 (paperback)
Subjects: Haxton, Naida J.
Women lawyers–Australia–Biography
Women editors–Australia–Biography
Lecturers–Australia–Biography
Dewey Number: 363.25092

Typeset in Minion Pro 12 pt.

Cover painting *Looking back on looking forward*, 2016 by Katerina Sakkas.

Printed and bound by Watson Ferguson & Company, Salisbury, Brisbane, Australia.

For my mother

Acquired/inherited philosophy/sayings

From my Mother
The only difference between a rut and a coffin is the dimensions.
Hating and negativity are a waste of energy.

From my husband
If you cannot say anything positive do not say anything at all.

Anonymous
If you need to say something negative or critical preface it by finding four good, praiseworthy things.

Contents

Acknowledgments

I spent many hours over the years since retirement thinking about how to record events in my life in a way that would be of interest to those who might read it. The first draft evolved with the title *I was* into lists of occupations I thought I had undertaken. It looked cumbersome and not right, so hence the approach adopted herein. While I have kept diaries and records of travel, etc, and quite a large quantity of material, there were many occasions when I needed help with my memory of events and details. There are many people to whom I am grateful for help, guidance and ideas and the following in particular:

My brother Jim for patiently triggering and correcting my memory of certain events and dates in family life;

Sue Wagner of Sue Wagner Books who read and wisely advised on my early drafts and on publishing matters;

The Hon J D Heydon AC QC for permission to quote from his farewell speech on my retirement;

The Hon David Hunt AO QC for permission to quote from correspondence from him;

The Bar Association of NSW for permission to use material in *Bar News*;

The Council of Law Reporting for NSW for permission to reproduce a headnote from 64 NSWLR 125;

The verifiers or research assistants, who responded with enthusiasm and generosity to a request to use material about them and, in the process, revived many useful memories;

Many friends who willingly provided input to material about them together with all of those whose names appear because their connections to me and the things I have done were enhanced by that connection;

Mike Gordon, my neighbour, skilled in photography, for the cover photo of the portrait by Katerina Sakkas;

Finally, the women from Haxton Chambers who triggered a serious start to actually writing the memoir.

Prologue

Diary of a 46th year (written at the time)

"Today I turned 46 years of age.

Turning any age or being any age has never particularly concerned me or worried me and being 46 seems no different to being 16 or 26 or 36 – all are ages of non-description, non-significance and non-celebratory events – but in the sequence of things numbers seem to count. In the sequence of my life at present 65 is almost the age of my husband, 14 is nearly the age of my son, my stepsons are maturing into their early thirties and producing little people of their own. For 21½ years I have pursued a career in the law. The year that marks this turning 46 is 1987.

And so my body is located in numbers and time but where is the person within the body to be located?

In terms of numerical years it feels ageless – it always has and it must communicate that feeling. My husband once gave as a reason for falling in love with me as being that I was ageless – and added somewhat enigmatically that if it had to be located in time it was probably best described as mid Victorian. My son with the confidence of his emerging and blossoming teens recognises each of my birthdays as a celebration of one year closer to dying.

In terms of practical living I am located in a large house with a large garden in a blissfully quiet non-suburb of the larger than life metropolis of Sydney. I have a home office and a city office for the pursuit of activities variously rewarded by monetary gains. I have material comforts and the maintenance thereof.

In terms of my personal development it can best be described as being – where this diary will spend a lot of its time I suspect – on a shelf waiting to be taken down and read, reread, completed, amended, altered, edited and hopefully …

At the age of 14 years my mother, in her wisdom, sent me to a girls' boarding school so that I might find out 'how girls behaved'. I had grown up in a family of boys in a country town abundantly endorsed with other families of boys. Consequently I had become very proficient at activities such as cricket, football, tennis, fishing and sailing. Surprisingly, I also became very proficient at cooking, knitting and sewing but then so to a degree did my brothers. There were occasions when the biological maleness within them reared its head and I was excluded from certain activities. There was the Christmas holiday when I was not allowed to be part of the camp at the bottom of the garden with all the male cousins and fancy-worked a full afternoon tea cloth and even crocheted the edge myself. There was a seventh birthday party of my elder brother when I was allowed to come only if I wore an apron and waited at the table.

Despite the fact that my mother believed and fostered the belief that we were all children and all equally so and all equally capable of achievement, I must be eternally grateful for the biological strength or weakness – whatever it might have been in those days – that sent me off to find out 'how girls behaved' and ensured me a good life in an interesting world but quite unintendedly in a world of males.

Out of those four years of finding out what was expected of girls, amongst a host of other good things, came each year at Christmas a card from my former headmistress. At Christmas 1986, her annual communication queried: 'how you and your ilk of this new generation of modern women manage to cope with such a full range of domesticity plus a career and especially plus the great challenge and satisfaction of nurturing not only the body but especially the mind and spirit of a teenage son with such wide ranging interests and bounding energy'.

To which I was prompted to reply that I had physically managed 'by juggling a little of this and a little of that – with the odd broken or inept routine – with a showman's smile – while the real me felt relegated to a shelf – like a good book or waiting, having been put aside, to be reached for whenever the opportunity arose'.

Her reply with the wisdom of experience in knowing and directing how girls behave says: 'I cannot assure you that you will find time to reach for that good book in the near future – but good books are good survivors too'."

And so, having survived now into my 8th decade, I think I may have been around long enough to take advantage of the opportunity and begin to explore and reflect upon my good life as a good book taken down from the shelf and not always spent on the shelf.

Why now?

Since I retired from practice at the Bar in NSW in 2006, people have asked: "Are you going to write your memoirs? – You must write your memoirs ..." At the official launch of *Haxton Chambers* in the Office of the DPP in Brisbane in 2006, the reason for naming the Chambers was stated by one young woman to be that I was regarded as a "hero". I made a promise to do something about telling "my story".

But how to do it?

In primary school we were taught that a story must have a beginning, a middle and an end. But there have been so many diversions and deviations in "my story" and my takings off the shelf that I felt overwhelmed by that approach and the confusion it might produce. Then I recalled a dear classmate from Somerville House, Roslyn Young, saying to me at about the time of our 45th year class reunion on her first return to Brisbane for many, many years: "When did you find time to sleep, with all those **things you have done**?" It was then that I realised that I had done many things and had indeed had a good life doing them. When I started to look through my papers I found much and a lot that I had forgotten (including the diary entry above) but had filed away under various headings. As a long-time editor and indexer of law reports and legal digests I began to see ideas for the outline, the headings and some of the content. And so it comes to fruition as ***Res Gestae – Things Done***. I have limited the topics to things done which have been significant to historical and social aspects of my time in history and my living in that time and for helping to create a rewarding life for me and hopefully for some others in those contexts.

We all see ourselves differently in time and space as do others who know us or know of us, which makes the task of writing this memoir, not only one of introspection but also one of self-observation. It has been quite challenging at times but with the help of trusted and true friends, many of whom are quoted herein, I hope I have found the right balance.

1. Things Educative

Things Educative — Learning — Primary and tertiary education — Teaching — Continuing education — Adult education — Summer Schools — Holidays — Travel — Familial education

That great man and relevantly great thinker, Abraham Lincoln, once said, in his first public speech to the people of Sangamon County, Illinois, on March 9, 1832, "Upon the subject of education … I can only say that I view it as the most important subject upon which we, as a people, can be engaged in …".

Reflecting upon those things which I have done I must agree. However one regards education and its many methods and/or philosophies, I feel in accord with Ruskin who expressed the thought in *Stones of Venice* in 1853 that "the training which makes men happiest in themselves also makes them most serviceable to others". I have loved and have been exceedingly content learning, being educated and acquiring knowledge, but especially imparting all that was gained in the process wherever I could.

When my formal education was finished and I had been practising at the Bar for a couple of months I was invited to be guest of honour at Somerville House Annual Speech Night on 30th November 1966 to make the Occasional Address and Distribute Prizes. In that address I said:

"Mr Chairman, Miss Taylor, Other Guests, Ladies and Gentlemen and Girls

May I say how deeply honoured I feel to have been asked to deliver the occasional address this evening. As you are now aware, it is a very short time ago that I was myself sitting down there somewhere, in a white dress and low heeled shoes. It is an even shorter time ago that I completed my formal education. Consequently, I am lacking in the wealth of worldly experience normally possessed by speakers on these occasions. You may therefore rightly wonder what qualifications I have to speak at all. My qualification appears to be that I have done something which has brought me publicity, attention, and a certain amount of curiosity, and you might think, glamour. That is not what I expected, not what I hoped, nor what I planned. Actually, I did something which I wanted to do, which I enjoyed doing and which I still enjoy.

What I am going to speak about this evening is not public or parental satisfaction but self-satisfaction, that stems perhaps from a philosophy of life. It was T S Eliot who said in 1932: 'To know what we want in education, we must know what we want in general. We must derive our theory of education from a philosophy of life'. I think most of you would acknowledge that it is very difficult indeed to have a complete philosophy of life while we are still proverbially schoolgirls. However, my contention is that a philosophy of life, to be meaningful, must be rewarding, and it cannot be rewarding if we are not allowed and encouraged to do what we want to do and what we like doing. Life is filled with a great deal more than qualifications and success, and the admonitions to give and share what is within us will be unnecessary, and the giving and sharing will come spontaneously if we are fully content with what we are doing and what we are getting from life in general.

It seems to be too often that parents and other well-intentioned persons offer advice, more particularly, to schoolgirls than schoolboys, as to what they should do to get on and this advice is based on their own philosophy of life, what they want or what they would like for their children. At the age when a girl is asked to choose what she wants in general — that is, by way of vocation — parental advice and encouragement are necessary and vital — but what is offered can quite often be greater discouragement than encouragement, and it is very difficult to disregard or contradict the advice of a successful parent, when obviously he or she must know what they are talking about: 'Father thinks I should do medicine because there are ample opportunities for women and my results in science are very good. I suppose I'll be able to keep up with history, which I like better in my spare time'. What is not realised is that the spare time is inevitably limited because the time involved in working industriously and contrary to inclination is far greater than the time spent working spontaneously. The other alternative is that children become enamoured with the idea of doing what Aunty Milly did or Cousin Kate mainly because they are very fond of the person in question, and without establishing whether they are really suited to that particular professional calling.

There is a great difference between working to get on and getting on with work. The progress of education is currently dominated by the idea of getting on. Undeniably, those with an education get on in our society but this attitude appears to me to have two fallacies: firstly, getting on or more particularly, efficiency and status are largely dependent on the will of the individual, and the rewards both materially and spiritually are greater if the individual is contributing all of himself and is both interested in and happy in contributing what is within himself.

The second fallacy is that school beyond a certain age is regarded as but a stepping stone to getting on in life, a place to do time until one can go to the university and become somebody, or do something. Unfortunately, very little water is sprayed on this attitude and one fails to recognise that, whilst being formally educated, one is still somebody and is still doing something. Had I been given any choice in coming here this evening, I should have preferred to be sitting down there wearing white. You may think that a strange preference for one who has so recently left school — for what after all could be better than to be in a similar position to the 70 odd girls for whom this evening is the end of school.

Unfortunately, it is not until we have finished with school and attempt to channel the qualifications that secondary education gives into a meaningful and satisfying occupation that we realise how much it means and how much it has to offer. It is not a prison in which we are doing time and from which we will suddenly be released into the world. It is part of the world and, more particularly, part of our world. We should therefore endeavour to make it as full and meaningful as possible. The opportunities we bypass in order to get somewhere as quickly as possible may never arise again. May I say to those of you who are still proverbially doing time: 'Take advantage of every opportunity that Somerville House offers. Your teachers and parents are not wardens. They are people who have developed their own philosophy of life, and are contributing towards your philosophy of life by giving of themselves; their dedication stems from the genuine interest in giving to each and every one of you the advantage of as wide a choice as possible. If you can reward their attention by being interested, for your own sake, the choice that you have to make will be a lot less difficult to make and should then be a choice which will satisfy yourself and give you happiness.'

You may well ask, what is happiness?

In the words of the current popular song: 'Happiness means different things to different people.'

In the words of the American cartoon character, Peanuts: 'Happiness is getting ten out of ten for spelling.'

May I leave you with the thought that happiness can be nine or even eight out of ten AND knowing you did it all yourself.

I hope that those of you who have made your choice will be happy in pursuing it and that those of you who have still to choose will be content with your ultimate choice."

Primary education

I started formal education in 1946 when I attended the Ballandean State Primary School in Prep 1. I knew nobody at the school except my older brother Jim. When I was not allowed to stand with him on parade and cried, the headmaster, from the heights of the verandah, called me a cry-baby. An hour or two later I was being upgraded because I could spell "sugar". The following year I was enrolled at Stanthorpe State Primary School in Prep 3. There I met my first great friend Helen Withers (now Burdett). How surprised I was to find her in my class when I arrived at Somerville House in 1956. We picked up where we had left off and still do wherever we are. In Auckland in 1948, I attended a primary school for most of the few months we were there but have no recollections whatsoever of that experience. On return to Australia in 1948 and resettling in Cleveland, I was enrolled at the Cleveland State Primary School in Grade 1, as it then was called. I can remember the other children at school saying how beaut it must be to have a mother who was a teacher and they would never believe that she did not help with homework, etc, and very rarely did she do so. Being a teacher she could hopefully and justifiably say — you go to school to learn; homework was only revision of what we should already know — and if she was going to do it for us, she'd go to school and get the rewards herself. Maybe she was an exceptional person and I regret that she did not get some of the rewards she missed out on in life. If we didn't understand she was there to explain but only after we had asked the teacher for an explanation first and still didn't understand. She was there to help find "sources", ideas and occasionally to check grammar or spelling but it was our work. She had a wonderful knack of deflecting some request for the impossible or unaffordable by telling us to come back when we had five good reasons why the request should be granted. We would not go back unless we could satisfy the condition. It was an early introduction to logic if nothing else. I remember (with embarrassment now) writing an essay at about the age of 10 on how I spent my Saturday mornings. One of my tasks was to scrub the loo — the earth closet type — wooden — up the backyard — and put in it something to the effect that is was "so clean you could eat your dinner off the seat (so said my mother)". She knew I had written it and she and the mistress had a good chuckle over it so I discovered later, but as a result of her commenting in the margin "really!", I learnt a little finesse. But then I was receptive to learning and many people it seems unfortunately are not.

The remainder of my primary education was completed at Cleveland State Primary School. By this time nothing could keep me away from school. I did not seem to have any problems with learning what was being taught or in reading beyond my age. I loved words and books. I spent time reading every suitable book in the local library and having to wait for the country extension delivery from the Brisbane Public Library before having something new to read. Maths seemed to be too easy at times. Consequently, as I grew older I was often sent to mind a class if the teacher was absent for any reason. I was 10 or 11 when one of the prep teachers was ill for three weeks and I was sent to "mind the class". Most of this involved supervising what the other prep teacher in the adjoining room set the class from time to time, listening to reading, reading stories and correcting writing, etc. I became so involved and enamoured that I took to wearing my Sunday-school clothes instead of my school clothes. We had sewing classes at which I had made by hand a simple top in cotton printed with butterflies, which I took to wearing. Sewing classes were very creative and very useful. We made samplers where we learned to hand sew all kinds of stitches and seams. When the task in hand was completed one could take over reading to the class. Here we were introduced to Dickens and other classical writers. I could not wait to have a turn. I loved reading and reciting aloud. My mother talked about elocution lessons but they were not available locally. I learned poems and recited at every opportunity including my mother's afternoon teas. At school we took part in lecturettes, which were very mini lectures on a given topic such as South Africa, kangaroos, sheep farming; it could be anything. Today it is called, I understand, a presentation and all forms of media are permitted. In class we created and solved crossword puzzles, played word games, learned the Greek and Latin roots for words, were sent up the street to stand on a specified corner and to come back to class and write a story — a composition — about what we saw or heard or imagined was going on. Mr T G Liesegang, the head-master, was a very creative and encouraging teacher. Out of class we looked after basic garden plots at school. We did physical education nearly every day, played handball, athletics, vigoro, basketball and tennis at every opportunity or played charades under a very large and shady tree when it was too hot. I took a shine to vigoro and taught myself to pitch down my arm to a pointing finger and hit the stumps with great success. There were inter-school competitions and matches which we all enjoyed.

In 1955, I represented the Redlands District in the State Primary School athletics championships.

In the 1950s the *Australian Woman's Mirror* ran a program called the Piccaninnies Corrobboree — whereby children could produce original works, drawings, crossword puzzles, verse and pars of some 100 words, all of which could be published. If published they earned cards with indigenous names such as Kurrajong, Budgeree and Mulga of varying points value. From the age of nine to the age of 13, I had 13 works published and advanced from member of Corroboree (MC) to distinguished member of Corroboree (DMC). The published items included this poem titled "Mickey the Roo":

Mickey was a kangaroo
Who lived next-door to us.
He never troubled anyone,
Or ever made a fuss.

He hopped about his yard all day
And sometimes all the night.
He liked to watch the children
But dogs gave him a fright.

He lived on tender grass shoots,
Or lettuce leaves so sweet.
Sometimes he had pudding,
Or biscuits for a treat.

And now I'm very sad to say
Poor Mickey is no more.
He got pneumonia one cold night
And died before the dawn.

I still have my membership badge with three little black dancing figures underneath the name — Piccaninnies Corroboree — in red.

There was only one radio for the whole family and we children were allowed to listen to The Argonauts on the ABC and sometimes to a play which was broadcast.

We rode our bikes to and from school and after school had play times with friends. One friend was the daughter of the local police sergeant and we often played in and around the courthouse including the courtroom. We learned to mend flat tyres and replace wandering chains. We swam and fished at every opportunity. Being a country town we all entered into community activities. I especially remember Sunday school as a place of joy and delighted in helping to provide and arrange the flowers on Saturday mornings with my cousin, and later, being a Sunday school teacher. I enjoyed Girl Guides, Red Cross and remember the whole town being involved in a pageant to celebrate the coronation of the Queen where, draped in plastic robes, I represented the Duchess of Gloucester.

I recall performing on stage in my early teens for a drama group which my mother helped direct; going to lectures by visiting academics in the local Memorial Hall; having my mind blown away by a lecture on the night sky; Anzac Day when the town all marched together; gardening. Having three brothers, I learned to play their way so as to be included and could probably still bowl overarm if need be. We played competition tennis. We swam, fished and rode bikes for miles. We holidayed with cousins on dairy properties and learned to ride horses. As a family we learned to work and play together. We entered anything we possibly could in the competitions in the local show. I gave up entering the children's cooking competition when my brother Jim won first prize for the sponge cake. Our mother had been a teacher for some 10 years before marrying, with most of the time spent at Cleveland and on the Darling Downs. Around 1952, married women who had been forced to leave the workforce on marriage were requested to come back into the Education Department because of the post-war baby boom. They were not allowed to teach at the same schools as their children initially, so when my mother went back to teaching at Thornlands, we became latchkey children and learned to do housework, to shop, to cook, to wash and iron. After a number of years she was appointed to Cleveland where she taught a second generation of children.

I grew up surrounded by encouragement to try, to do and to challenge oneself and to be morally good. Every new challenge or encounter brought something or somebody, which I **then** wanted to pursue or be. I was lucky to be fairly good at most things I tried. To this day, I still love pursuing the new challenge or encounter: philosophy because I never did it at Uni; watercolour painting; hieroglyphics after travelling to Egypt; courses on anything I have not done before.

In 1955, I sat for the Queensland State Scholarship examination, which allowed passage from primary to secondary school, obtaining an average pass across the three subjects (English, Mathematics (for which I got 100%)

and Social Studies) of 93%. This placed me approximately eleventh in the State. Mr Liesegang was my teacher during scholarship year.

Secondary education

And so to secondary school. My mother, who had gone to State High in South Brisbane, was determined that I should go to a girls' school and find out how girls behaved (having grown up in what was then a country town with a horde of boys). And so I went to Somerville House in Brisbane in 1956 and as a boarder in 1957 only, though Miss Taylor was very kind in the final two years in allowing me to sleep in the hospital when it was difficult to get home to Cleveland. In memory of my mother, I should say that I am most grateful that she insisted on my going to Somerville and thereby introduced me to such wonderful people and experiences. It was here that I could be introduced to Art of Speech which my mother had always referred to as elocution. After I left school I completed a teaching qualification, ATCL (Speech and Drama) (Associate of Trinity College London), which provided me with much needed funds for a number of years while at the university.

The whole experience of being part of an all girls' school where, as I recall it, every encouragement was given to independence in thought, action, creativity and self-discipline was a powerful influence. The School motto was and is, "Honour before Honours", and that was the ethic that we lived and breathed. I actually enjoyed the discipline of teachers like Miss McCallum (Maths) and Miss George (French) because it pushed one further than expected. I loved Art of Speech with Miss Wheller and am sure she played a big part in my English results. Contrary to many in the school, I got on well with Miss Taylor (Headmistress) and stayed friends with her until she died. I wish someone had kept her morning devotions.

As a daygirl, I travelled by train from Cleveland to Vulture Street Station (now South Bank) each day. This involved steam trains and rail motors, often changing trains at Manly. Each trip could take just under an hour. Time was not for wasting and on board, homework was done using the top of the school case as a desk, jumpers were knitted and books were read. Participation in school sports and practice for inter-House events meant the days could be very long. Strangely I do not recall being tired or bored.

Life as a boarder for one year was a different and rewarding experience. Here, I had time to make lasting friendships and to enjoy living without boys around. Here were surroundings in which I could dream of being a lawyer so the subjects I undertook were geared to law and, as a backup, teaching. Latin at Junior level was then a requirement for entry to law. Maths was still an easy subject for me and when a lovely Chinese/Malaysian student Tan Suan Cheng (Sue to us) arrived in the boarding school with Maths slightly behind the class standard, Miss McCallum asked me to help her at the weekends and provided me with the material to do so. We spent Saturday mornings under the boarding school working our way through the material provided. I also recall a time when I was asked to supervise a lower class in Mathematics when the mistress was unavoidably away. Teaching did seem to be in the blood.

During my four years at Somerville House I was a member of the school athletics team taking part in the GPS athletics each year and winning a half pocket and three bars. I was a member of the Macarthur House Committee. In my senior year at the school I was promoted to Prefect and Chief Reference Librarian, the latter a role that involved dusting shelves, mending books and generally helping out in the library. We spent hours after school at the South Brisbane Library then across Vulture Street from the school where we learned some of the skills required for mending books.

In 1957, I sat what was then known as the Junior Examination gaining five As and four Bs. This result provided a junior scholarship to the Teachers' Training College. In 1959, I gained five As and two Bs in the Senior examination winning both a Commonwealth Scholarship and a State Secondary School Teacher's Scholarship for one year at the University of Queensland. With a Commonwealth Scholarship I was then able to choose Arts/Law as my degrees, repay the teaching scholarship but also remain very mindful of having a fall-back position if law as an occupation did not eventuate. At the Matriculation ceremony in the University of Queensland quadrangle there was something like 40 Somerville House girls in attendance. We were, in retrospect and without knowing it, an exceptionally bright year as our Junior and Senior results had demonstrated. We had educated and stimulated each other quite unwittingly and were taking it all on further with the bonus of the self-motivation nurtured at Somerville.

Tertiary education

As the St Lucia campus was too difficult to attend as a day student from Cleveland where a bus service was programmed to replace the train service to Brisbane, I became a "living away from home" resident of Milton House, a Presbyterian Hostel for Ladies at Milton. In 1961, I was Secretary of the students club and, in 1962, I was President. In both positions I represented Milton House on the Inter-College Council of the University Colleges: I hosted balls and social events: I was a member of the Milton House athletics team, competing in the inter-college athletics competition. In 1963 I was Senior Student during my first year of Articles. The role of senior student included standing in for the principal at breakfast prayers and generally being available to help younger students. It also involved being responsible for locking the doors at the appropriate time to ensure that all students were in on time and all visitors were out on time. Today that would probably be called mentoring. For three of those years I augmented my scholarship fees by teaching speech to younger children in Brisbane and surrounding districts and coaching mathematics for which I had obtained 100% pass marks at all secondary school examinations.

I then moved into what would be called a studio apartment in Auchenflower near the train station for the final two years of university combined with work as an Articled Clerk.

In 1965 I captained the Queensland University team in the intervarsity moots (mock trials) in Canberra. It appears from available records that I was the first female student from UQ to participate in intervarsity moots.

From 1960 to 1965 I debated for both the Young Liberals and the Milton House Student Club taking part in and adjudicating for the Queensland Debating Union A Grade Championships. For many years I debated with Kathy Martin (later Kathy Sullivan AM), Robert Banner and Colin Bird (later Lamont). Debating was one activity where one researched and acquired knowledge on matters outside the degree curriculum.

Lecturing

Before the end of my first year at the Bar I was invited to become and appointed as a part-time lecturer in Land Law in the Faculty of Law at the University of Queensland and subsequently invited by the Commerce Faculty to become and was formally appointed a part-time lecturer in Commercial Law. Preparing and delivering lectures was another learning experience that required staying up to date and that was to stand me in good stead for the rest of my career. And so lecturing in legal subjects began another thing to do and is detailed more fully in ***Things Legal.***

Continuing Education

All of which brings me to my own continuing education which has never stopped but has certainly expanded in subjects and depth. Keeping up with the law was just an inherent part of legal practice. There was a life outside law. In whatever you do there is always something new.

I was always an avid reader on any topic that took my fancy. I would, and still do, go to the library with a list of fiction writers that might have interested me and maybe a non-fiction title or two but some of the most interesting books I have devoured and frequently acquired were those on the new books stand where the topic intrigued me. One is often asked — what is the book that has had the most influence on you or what book has changed your life? I have never quite understood what those kinds of questions really seek as an answer.

I can, however, say that the book that has had the most significant impact on my life is a dictionary that was handed down to me by a family member when I was 12 years old. It has long lost its original bindings and cover pages so I cannot give its provenance. It is still on my library shelf and still used frequently. What was its impact? For nearly every word in this dictionary it gives a Latin or Greek derivative — as well as its meaning. Looking up words became an exciting and stimulating exercise. When a major spelling bee was held across Queensland in the 1950s and came to Cleveland where I lived, my friend Margaret Power and I decided it would help us if we read our dictionaries. She had a pocket OED. So, after school most days, we climbed to the top of a large custard-apple tree on her family farm and read our dictionaries sustained by freshly picked, ripe custard-apples. Words, their meaning, emphases, origins and connections became part of my living and working life — Somerville, UQ, BA with English major, LLB, Teaching Diploma in Speech and Drama, Debating, Mooting, Professional Ethics, letter writing and Law Reporting, plus the thrill of finding new words and collecting new dictionaries and new word books. From then on my reading list became very eclectic — one book leading to another. It still does. As I write this there is frequently more than one dictionary open on the dining room table. Books are where ideas come from.

In 1994, I started to record selectively notes of those books I had read. It rather petered out at the end of 2014 and as I finish this I have renewed the habit. I have included a few samples along the way as new interests entered my life.

1985 was the first year since 1966-67 that I travelled overseas and that was to Europe and UK with husband David and son James. We went again in 1988 to UK only. Here I found another world of things to learn about and do. What a treasure trove. Sometime after returning, friends talked about a trip they had done to the Cambridge Summer School and what a great experience it had been. I tucked that away in my list of things to do one day. In the meantime the University of New South Wales, AGSM, had advertised a one year graduate diploma in professional ethics for which I had enrolled but the course was cancelled for lack of interest and hopefully postponed for another time. I had added professional ethics to the list.

The day for Cambridge came in 1993, when I agreed to accompany my sister-in-law to a Cambridge Summer School and set about looking at what courses I could do. Son James had just started Arts at Sydney University and was enamoured of philosophy. As I had never done philosophy and it tied in with ethics, philosophy became my choice for the Summer School, with the selection of subjects being moral philosophy and modern philosophy. On arrival I was informed that I could do another subject in the afternoon and made a choice for something less erudite (I thought) in The History of the English Country House. So there I was in a student room in Selwyn College, three meals a day in Hall, and more amazing stimulating things to do and about which to learn than I could possibly have imagined. A one to one with the lecturer, Alan Hobbs, over morning tea established my status in the course as someone seeking an introduction to the subject and a reading list to take home. I did not wish to take away any kind of certificate: I simply wanted further information that I could pursue at home. There were other morning tea chats on all sorts of topics. I did enjoy his assessment of the 20th century condition as one of "rootlessness and combative rhetoric". The afternoon lectures were an eye-opener to both art and architecture delivered most enthusiastically and practically. The class would frequently adjourn to the Fitzwilliam Museum to look closely at something on display. Daily suggestions were made as to places to visit or things that were on, eg, evensong at Ely Cathedral, a short trip away. We were guided to Stamford with its stone village and streets, to Norwich Cathedral for the wonderful bosses, to Belton House with a home library to die for.

Then we went to London, to a corner apartment in Pimlico, from which I swallowed Bloomsbury, the Galleries, the Houses of Parliament and where a visit to the Victoria and Albert Museum with a newly acquired list of things to see had become a must. As I walked around I kept meeting this sign that said "Summer School this way". Another thing to do and so onto the wish list it went with all the information I could get from Administration.

In November 1993, David was diagnosed with pancreatic cancer and was advised that it was terminal. Life took a tumble and a different kind of learning kicked in. With the help and advice of a very pragmatic specialist, a practical caring GP and some wonderful palliative care nurses we set about living what was left the best way we could. He died at home in June 1994. We had planned to go to Alaska this year. I calculate that I devoted about 25 hours a week to being married and needed to fill those hours, so set about doing so.

1995 sees the Graduate Diploma in Professional Ethics happen. Here I am at UNSW on Monday nights at 6 pm with three other mature students and often more lecturers, tutors and visitors than students. A Board table, a plate of sandwiches and coffee and the evenings flowed with demanding topics and conversations. I produced papers on topics such as *Ethics is Not an Option for Business, Ethics — A Paradigm for Skilful Thinking,* the model for which I tested for usefulness on university students in the School of Philosophy, and *A Candidate of Good Fame and Character — What Characteristics Make a Good Lawyer*? and *The Ethics of Complaining.* I was encouraged to attend the lectures on Aristotle in the Philosophy Department. I acquired four large binders of reading material which took me in never ending directions.

So, in 1995, I am heavily into morals, ethics, philosophy and beginning to investigate topics such as thinking and corporate governance. Some titles: *Just friends, The Role of Friendship in our Lives*, by Lillian B Rubin; *The Perfect Negotiation* by Gavin Kennedy.

In 1997, I take an apartment in South Kensington around the corner from the Victoria and Albert Museum (V&A), having enrolled in a three week Summer School on Art and Architecture of the West. Not previously knowing the difference between a Doric or Corinthian column, a whole new world of archaeology as well as architecture and art opened up. Mornings were devoted to lectures and afternoons to gallery tours. As there are something like 204 galleries in the V&A, we were daily given a choice of two out of three and conducted around by one of the lecturers. We were also given details of other galleries and places to visit, books to read and acquire. When I kept asking questions about how things were done, eg, illuminated manuscripts or stone cathedrals, a kindly lecturer sent me off to the children's section of the National Gallery bookshop with a list of what to look for. How simple it all seemed when explained for little people. Evenings were spent at the theatre or just up the road at concerts in the Royal Albert Hall, to which a kind Londoner doing the course offered tickets from time to time.

The knowledge acquired to this point meant there were many allied or new avenues to explore. When the NSW Art Gallery magazine arrived, I would look closely at the lectures and book for those in which I might be interested: *Oh My God; Sicily; Civilisations.* Four times a year there appeared, and continues to appear, with the daily newspaper a booklet from WEA Sydney outlining the courses for the particular quarter of the year — Spring, Summer, Autumn or Winter. I wind my way through every catalogue which arrives highlighting courses or one-off sessions that might interest me. Across the years I have chosen to do and enjoyed courses on watercolour painting, drawing with pastels, drawing on the right side of the brain, drawing trees, Italian for travellers, Egypt, Hieroglyphics, Sicily, Financial Management, Gi Gong, Turkey, how to write a play, creative writing, and in more recent times androids for seniors. I discovered an eight week course in the continuing education department of the University of Sydney on the philosophy of travel and found the topic most intriguing, thought provoking and engaging. In retirement I have become an addict of the ABC Radio National programs and many BBC programs.

Add to this the travel and holiday experiences detailed in ***Things Peripatetic*** and one can only agree with Abraham Lincoln's view that education is the most important activity in which we can be engaged. I have never been disappointed in the time spent or in the knowledge acquired. I go on, and will go on, looking and hoping to find something interesting to learn about by doing.

Familial education

I was not the only one in the family to benefit from things educative in growing up as we did as a family, in the learning experiences that came with it, in encouragement to do well and to make our own choices and in using what we learned to give back to community.

Brother Jim followed our mother into teaching. He completed his primary and secondary education at Wynnum High and Intermediate School obtaining a Scholarship to the Teachers Training College in Brisbane. He taught at Capalaba for a year and then went to one teacher schools on the

Darling Downs and in North Queensland. He was headmaster at Pinnacle then Stuart Primary School in Townsville for a number of years and retired from Home Hill after 15 years there when the trials and tribulations of administration made inroads into what he really liked doing and that was teaching. He always took time to be involved in local community activities such as Rotary, Probus, junior tennis, cricket and basketball. For three years he was president of Life Education NQ. He was much loved by pupils and parents and is still invited back to umpire at the Vigoro championships in North Queensland. He retired to Buderim where he has continued to learn, to teach and to be involved in his communities. He designed digital learning programs for his grandchildren, attends the local school to help with literacy, became involved with Friendship Force Australia on the Sunshine Coast, designed their website, presided over their travels and homestays for a number of years and was awarded a Wayne Smith Medal for services to Friendship Force.

Brother David was not so keen on structured learning. He frustrated our mother no end by such things as referring to Richard II as King Dick and preferring to do anything else but his homework. He spent some time at Slade School in Warwick because of his asthma and, after the Junior Exam, took up an apprenticeship in the Australian Army. The Australian Army had commenced an Apprentice scheme in August 1948 at Balcombe Barracks on the Mornington Peninsula in Victoria. To train tradesmen and women direct from Australian secondary schools, youths aged between 14 and 18 were recruited for a four-year apprenticeship in various technical and clerical trades. Sapper Haxton became an apprentice in electrical trades. When qualified he was the one to head to various sites to set up camp electrics before the troops arrived. He got to work on Cape York before bomb testing, Borneo where road building was taking place and Papua New Guinea for infrastructure works. He left army life for life as an electrician. With an autistic son, he involved himself in disability care and services and became a regular at Rotary where he was awarded the Paul Harris Fellow for Services to Rotary. He is a keen organiser of reunions of the Balcombe boys.

Brother Harry finished secondary education at Slade School in Warwick, did Economics and was one of the first students in the first Post Graduate Diploma in Information Processing (1970) at Queensland University and worked at a bank and in a finance company before starting a business in records management which involved filing, storage, archiving and advising. He lectured and wrote courses, textbooks and manuals in Records Management (RM) for TAFE and university level for many years. He spent some 12 years developing computer software for records management before moving into the outsourcing of RM services, which he remained in until retirement. He was the Inaugural National Secretary, later National President and State President of the Records Management Association of Australia (now Records Information Professionals Australasia (RIMPA)) and was made an Honorary Life Member in 1985. In May 2016, RIMPA Queensland Branch inaugurated the Harry Haxton Shield Award for Individual Achievement. Harry and partner, Peg, developed a business supplying materials to preserve works of art on paper, supplying all major galleries and museums in Australasia. He was made an Honorary Life Member of the AICCM (Australian Institute for the Conservation of Cultural Materials) in 1987. In 2002, he was interviewed as part of the Oral History of Australia as being one of the significant persons in the development of Conservation in Australia. With sight in one eye only his involvement with sport was on the side-lines but not just as a spectator. He sponsored NBL and State basketball and became Club President and Honorary Member, with a particular interest in State level competitions and women's basketball.

And so I have chosen to do many things along the education pathway. I take you back to the introduction above and my use of the word "choice" in relation to one's education and careers. The word choice is an interesting word, usually representing freedom and independence to choose. The topic of choice has been endlessly discussed in relation to women, the feminist movement, bad choices to which are often attributed unhappiness, uninformed consents, misrepresentation and coercion. Unfortunately not all of the choices we make can be attributed to the same forces. Choice can refer to:

- the act of choosing
- the power of choice, election or preference
- the care or discrimination in choosing (involving judgement or skills)
- the number of things proposed or offered for selection
- the thing chosen.

Feminists have been inclined to regard choice as a means of empowerment. The right choice may well be empowering and a means to many things, but in reality the choices we make are shaped by, amongst other things, our backgrounds, our personal strengths and weaknesses, our skills, our likes and dislikes, our commitment and resilience and no doubt the financial rewards to be derived therefrom. We may not see it at the time we make a choice but it would seem also to spawn responsibility to those around us, to the thing chosen and to ourselves in terms of the happiness it will bring us.

Naida Jean, not yet 2, Oct 1943, dressed for an outing

Naida about 10 years old wearing Red Cross uniform outside Cleveland house.

In uniform of Girl Guides beside the banana trees at Cleveland aged about 12.

The compulsory photo on visiting Lone Pine Koala Sanctuary.

At the desk in Grade 5 at Cleveland State School when the school photographer came.

1956 in brand new Somerville House summer uniform beside the frangipani tree at Cleveland.

Cleveland State School as it was in 1955. I occupied the room on the left for a couple of years. After I went to High School, my mother came back to teach at Cleveland and was dropped at the front gate each morning where there were always a number of adoring pupils waiting to carry her bag.

Somerville House Boarders in Junior year. Naida front row left and Sue Tan front row right.

2. Things Legal

Things Legal — Influences — Law School — Debating — Moots — Articles of clerkship — Practice — Law reporting — Entrepreneuring — Project management — Legal education — Mentoring — Publications — Voluntary contributions — Regrets and disappointments — Honours

What does **doing** law involve? After I graduated in law I became aware that the Women Graduates Association of the University of Queensland had started a careers advisory evening which was conducted in the Brisbane City Hall once a year. Each discipline was allocated a booth and people from various professions were available to provide information to high school students. I was invited to participate. How does one introduce a high school student to a career in the law? How does one describe a career in the law, a law degree or what it can be used for? A law degree quite obviously required and still requires good English skills, hopefully logic, an ability to read, retain and apply masses of material, good communication skills and maybe an interest in history. Some experience in public speaking or debating might be regarded as essential. The usual outcomes were seen to be to become a solicitor or barrister or join a public service as a prosecutor or legislative draftsman. The prevailing concept seemed to be that one would start at the bottom and end up at the top as a partner, a judicial officer or silk, the DPP or Parliamentary Draftsman. The requirements may not have changed but the possibilities certainly have. Today a graduate can have one career or a portfolio of careers or can specialise in a particular area of the law. Even as a barrister I was able to be versatile in where I put my energies but it did not mean that they led to elevation to judicial office.

Early interest in Law

Where I grew up in Cleveland we lived very close to the local police station and courthouse and passed it regularly. Part of living in a country town was being on friendly terms with the local police officers who would happily collect you and your bicycle with the flat tyre in the back of the jeep and take you home. Two of them, Sergeant James and Constable Hedley Nichol (who subsequently disappeared on a catamaran in the Pacific), had children with whom we became friendly and consequently we played in the police yard and buildings. I was intrigued by the courtroom and wanted to know what went on there to a point where they promised to come and get me the next time the magistrate was sitting. They kept their word and changed my life. I wanted to be that person. But, my family was not wealthy and I continued to believe that I would be a teacher.

I have dealt with my secondary education at Somerville House in ***Things Educative***. Here we were encouraged to believe in ourselves, to challenge ourselves, to be independent and to do "good". When I did win both a State Secondary Teacher's Scholarship and a Commonwealth Scholarship, I was faced with a choice in which my then widowed mother encouraged me. The choice was to take the Commonwealth Scholarship and do Arts/Law with the safety net that, if law was not feasible as a career, there was always teaching with an Arts degree. And so I approached six busy, wonderful years at the University of Queensland.

University and Arts/Law

The Queensland University campus was a much smaller place than it is now and we were lucky enough to be able to continue friendships with people who were not necessarily in our faculty and to join cross-faculty clubs. The public transport to Cleveland was not ideal and so I attended Milton House, a college run by the Presbyterian Church at McDougall

Street, Milton. I was, in turn, Secretary and President of the Student Club and represented the College on the Inter-College Council of University Colleges. In my final year, I became what was known as Senior Student with the role of mentoring other students. On campus, I joined the Drama Society and took part in a couple of plays, the Political Science Club, the Evangelical Union, the Debating Society, for which I both debated and adjudicated, and the Law School Moots in which I participated. I joined the Women's Cricket Club but found it too difficult to get to practice and gave up. At Milton House I regularly did Meals on Wheels for St Andrew's Church. It was a very busy and challenging time. I used to travel home to Cleveland most weekends, often to sew up a dress for the next ball or social outing and to teach maths and speech to young people in the district to supplement my scholarship living allowance.

Off campus, I joined Young Liberals with Kathy Martin (Sullivan, who was a friend from school and later became a Senator for Queensland and an MHR for Moncrieff on the Gold Coast) and mainly because it provided a different opportunity to debate, which we did for a number of years. On campus, I enjoyed most subjects and loved Legal History and Land Law where we were lectured by the wonderfully knowledgeable Professor Walter Harrison. Whilst I never thought I got great marks, I was, in later years, asked by Professor Tarlo to come back onto campus to teach his classes in Land Law when he first arrived at the University, "because of your results". I later taught the subject in Sydney. I recall Criminal Law, with John Morris, where things seemed more logical than other subjects, Constitutional Law with Daryl Lumb where we once turned up for a Friday night lecture all dressed to go out in ball gowns and black tie, Industrial Law with Professor Sykes, contracts with Bruce McPherson (later McPherson JA) who failed half the class for not distinguishing mistake from fundamental breach, Practice and Procedure and Ethics (with judges and senior barristers as lecturers) at the Supreme Court at 8 am in the morning. We had a very varied and broad curriculum and we didn't talk about or even think about, as far as I recall, specialising in any particular area of the law. We learned a lot about general principles, and I think that's one reason I ended up where I did end up in Law Reporting because not too many people today are generalists in the legal fraternity. University students today seem to decide as they enter a law degree in what area of law they are going to be specialising. And then there was the Law Library, which you were allowed to enter only in second year and where you could smoke. Heaven forbid! I smoked my pipe in there once for a £5 dare. One was not awarded honours in the 1950s or 1960s but had to earn them by doing an additional year and writing a thesis. This was an additional expense. Six years without an income is a long time and there was pressure to get Articles and to move on.

After the end of first year in Arts, we started law subjects and from this time on, I was joined in most classes by Frances Cleary (Blok), Quentin Strachan (Bryce) and later, Joan Behm (Bennett) who joined us from the fledgling University of Townsville. There were a number of women in various other years in the Law Faculty at the time including Margaret Kelly, who became a partner at John P Kelly & Co, Mary Foley (Finn), Brigidine Behan and Elizabeth Gill. What is interesting about the times is that from 1938 to 1965 there are only 10 female graduates from the Law School and only five of those were admitted as Barristers. I was the first to actually go into practice in 1966 and it was not until 1975 that Susan Kiefel (now Justice Kiefel AC of the High Court) became the next woman to go into practice.

In May 1963, I was admitted to the Degree of Bachelor of Arts, having majored in English.

I acquired many friends at university and in college, not all law students. I do recall we were intent on getting qualified and getting work and having a good time. I learned how to put in an appearance at the "Law Smokos" and disappear after two drinks before the night got too advanced. We all knew each other and had a lot of fun together. But there were really very few of us when you consider the number of students in the Law faculty as I write this. Our graduation class in 1965 was only 19 of which three were women. Leo Williams introduced me to Rugby Union by insisting that I came to inter-faculty games and barrack for the Law Faculty. He also took me to a memorable game between South Africa and Australia at Lang Park in 1963. He was one of the many people who became friends and made sure that I did not miss out on anything. I remember him with much gratitude for taking me to Princess Alexandra Hospital after night lectures to visit my sick mother and waiting to take me home to Auchenflower.

Articles of clerkship

Pat Garde, who was a conveyancer in Queen Street, Brisbane and who knew Norman Dean who had been an army friend of my father and who lived in Cleveland, took up the challenge of helping me to find Articles. He approached Miss Elizabeth Hart of Flower and Hart; I was interviewed and, in the language of the day, was indentured. I do not recall anything about that interview. Teaching as a career then disappeared. Three years of working and attending university at the same time was hard work. I learned so much at Flower and Hart that was basic and disciplined and has stood me in good stead throughout my career. I learned to pick up a pencil and make notes when the phone rang and to use a dictaphone efficiently. The articled clerks each had a foolscap book with duplicating paper in which we entered details of our telephone contacts and later cut them into strips and pasted them on to the client's costs sheet. I now dictate directly to the computer with a wonderful speech recognition system. How much the life of a lawyer has changed and how much more efficient it has become. I still pick up a pen when the phone rings. I learned about accuracy and clarity of expression especially as the articled clerks were expected to check the typing with the secretaries. This entailed sitting down together and one reading aloud to the other. Many years later at sports matches at Shore Playing Grounds at Northbridge in Sydney, I kept looking at another woman and trying to work out from where I knew that face. When I finally struck up the courage to ask, it turned out that she had been Miss Hart's secretary for a number of years. No wonder I knew the face. I had sat opposite it so often in checking typing. When it came to the exam for legal drafting the words came almost automatically from my pen. I learned about costs and accounting: we were expected to prepare a draft of our own costs. I spent six months with the search clerk, for which I was forever grateful when giving an advice on evidence. I knew what to ask for and how realistic it was to obtain. Miss Hart taught us to be careful to the point of pedantry, to prepare well and not be overawed by clerks behind counters. If sent to find out about something from, eg, the Stamp Duties Office, you would not dare to come back with half an answer even if it meant sitting around for ages waiting to see someone more senior than the counter clerk. I enjoyed the company of the other articled clerks, Tony Brown, William Hart and Michael Meadows even though they were inclined to be teasers and could lock me in the strong room if they passed the door when I was looking for something inside. There was a lot of hard work as well as good natured fun as the following *Ode to a Cigarette Bum* written in 1963 to a fellow articled clerk suggests:

Dear Sir
Your efforts at disguise
Are seen by many eyes

You wander around and hum
In manner of many a bum,
You fidget and you squirm
Like every good weed worm,
Your actions are ignored
And placidly deplored
You think that you are bright
But unaware of quite
The effect you are creating
You go on debating
Whether to continue your actions
With perhaps dissatisfaction
Or stop where you rest
And go test
Other mugs like me
Who without forgiving
But with much misgiving
Indulge your whim
To be consequently thought dim-
Witted, who for the sake of propriety
And a feeling that society
Has had a sufficient upheaval
Not to add another weevil
To the battlefields of scum
Like you, you bum!
How I wish you were a dumper dead
That I could grind into the ground, instead
Of saying
Politely
And very nicely
No, no do not fret
Would you care for a cigarette?

Max Lockhart was exceedingly patient in getting us to write letters of advice on a matter, allowing time for research and then going through the result and producing lucid and much shorter explanations. Miss Hart was more than generous with her time and patience and often took me to dinner at Rowe's Restaurant when I had stayed behind to get assignments done. The firm was very happy to allow the clerks to use the library out of hours. This was a great bonus, when at the end of the day one did not have to go out to the campus at St Lucia to get access to law reports. Ailsa Heathwood, who had been articled to Miss Hart in the 1950s, returned from a working holiday in London and helped with the training of the articled clerks. There was really no time to sit and contemplate our situation in life or our futures. One got on with getting things done. I do not recall anyone as being a "role model". The goal was to become gainfully employed using our qualifications.

Encouragement to go to the Bar

I captained the team for the Intervarsity Moots in Canberra in 1965. I believe, from available Law School records, that I was the first female student to participate in Intervarsity Moots in the faculty. Sir Garfield Barwick, who was then Chief Justice of the High Court, presided at our first moot as Chair of a fictional ACT Court, the material for which involved damages for negligence in relation to a boating accident on Lake Burley Griffin, which was Commonwealth territory. When I stood up to open, he asked the question: "Now, Miss Haxton, what jurisdiction do we have to hear this case?" A question never forgotten and to be first ascertained when any brief turned up on my desk. At related social events Sir Garfield and other academics took me aside and encouraged me to contemplate going to the Bar. In December of 1965, I was admitted to the degree of Bachelor of Laws.

Towards the end of my term of articles I was also actively encouraged by David Jackson and Ian Gzell and others to consider joining them at the Bar. The major issue, as it still is, was getting suitable chambers. It was quietly known that a set of chambers was likely to become available at the end of the year. The availability of chambers was a very galvanising point. I set some plans in motion.

I completed my Articles of Clerkship in March of 1966 and was entitled to be admitted to practise as a Solicitor of the Supreme Court of Queensland. There was a clause in the Articles of Clerkship which provided that at the expiration of the term of the clerkship I should continue to "serve as a clerk" for a further term of three years or "during such part thereof as the Master Solicitor should desire the service of [myself] at a remuneration to be determined being not less than the minimum salary that a law clerk should during such period be entitled to receive under any then existing award of the Arbitration Court having relation to law clerks or under any then existing law or regulation thereunder". When I asked my Master Solicitor if I could be released from the obligations under that clause as at the end of 1966 because I wished to go to the Bar rather than be a solicitor and that there was a real possibility that suitable Chambers would be available at the end of the year, I was peremptorily dismissed. I was asked to leave on Friday. I would be breaking my contract and this was unforgiveable.

Pre-admission

I could not be admitted to the Bar immediately as I had not complied with all the rules or some of the rules relating to the admission of Barristers of the Supreme Court of Queensland in relation to time to be served as a student-at-law prior to admission. I was indeed lucky to find a position as a locum in the Brisbane office of Clive Wyman & Co whilst Mr Wyman was overseas. I appreciated the confidence which Mr Wyman placed in me and enjoyed the challenges and responsibilities of this positon. Not only did I learn much about running a small practice but I gained an insight into and experience in dealing directly with staff. I recall making an early decision that it was important in terms of gaining respect that I dressed more professionally than the staff and kept it in mind at future times.

During this time I became aware from conversations with junior members of the Bar recently admitted that there was a set of Chambers which would be available towards the end of 1966 which then belonged to Bernard Goldberger who was leaving the Queensland Bar to go and live in Sydney. After discussions and negotiation it was agreed that I could purchase Goldberger's Chambers and join a group of barristers including David Jackson, Ian Gzell, Des Draydon and Con McLaughlin. It proved difficult to get finance without a male guarantor but the Commonwealth Bank agreed to a $500 overdraft on a life insurance policy with just over two years on the clock.

As no woman had previously practised at the Bar in Queensland enquiries were made as to what was the appropriate clothing to be worn by a female barrister in court. The Honourable Justice Gibbs, prompted by his then Associate, Des Draydon, researched the matter as much as he was able and came up with a description of bar jacket, wings and collars, and "shoes with buckles". The French shoes with buckles were a very good buy as they are still in very wearable condition. Roma Mitchell, then a barrister and solicitor of the South Australian Supreme Court, when asked for advice, wrote stating that on occasions when one needed to go to court a hat was essential. Janet Coombs, then of the New South Wales Bar, wrote explaining what was worn by herself and one other member of the New South Wales Bar at the time, including diagrams and drawings of collars with wings and bands. Out of all of this, and taking into account the perceived requirement to share a robing room with the all-male Bar, I had designed and made a black suit the jacket of which, when worn under robes, presented as a bar jacket but was suitably styled so as to be worn in the street and look like a suit. In 1966 barristers did not appear in public places wearing wigs and gowns as is now done. I decided that unrobed appearances should be hatless and never wore a hat to court.

Admission

On 30 August 1966, before a Bench consisting of Gibbs J, Lucas J and Douglas J, I was admitted to the Queensland Bar.

I had asked the Court to waive compliance with the rules relating to the admission of Barristers of the Supreme Court of Queensland in relation to time to be served as a student-at-law prior to admission as a barrister. I had completed all other requirements under the *Rules Relating to the Admission of Barristers* then in force. These Rules required one to be registered as a student-at-law for 15 months and to attend the hearing of and write and submit for the approval of the Barrister's Admission Board something like 10 reports on various proceedings of the courts. I had complied with the provisions as to writing reports and had been a student-at-law for 13 months. I was anxious that the day in Court would not be wasted. While robing in the room of one of the Associates, I was told "not to worry, they have written their decision already". That decision, which exempted me from further compliance with the particular Rule as to time is reported in the Queensland Law Reporter as *Re Haxton* [1966] QWN 36.

The *Courier-Mail* reported the proceedings thus:

> "At yesterday's sittings of the Full Court, Mr Justice Gibbs congratulated Miss Haxton on her admission as a Barrister.
>
> He said: 'You are the first of many women who will in time undoubtedly practise at our Bar.
>
> I think it is nearly 40 years since a woman was first admitted to the Queensland Bar.
>
> Although women have long practised with success as solicitors in Queensland, you will, if you carry out your present

> intention, be the first woman to engage in private practice as a barrister in this State.
>
> In this respect, we in Queensland have been behind the trend of the times. …
>
> In some of the other States as in England, women have achieved eminence in practice at the Bar."

My admission was moved by C E K Hampson later QC (who was to be my master in the master/pupil relationship at the Bar during my first year). He resurfaced in my life as Chair of the Consultative Council of Law Reporting Bodies with which I became involved after moving to NSW. We stayed in touch until after he had retired.

Rules for admission to the Bar around Australia have changed considerably (and for the better) especially after a nationwide requirement was set for practising certificates to be held in the mid-1990s. There are, for example, now five prerequisites for practising at the Bar in NSW:

- Admission as a lawyer in an Australian jurisdiction
- Passing the NSW Bar Examination to the required standard
- Completion of an application for an Australian practising certificate, with conditions attached
- Completion of the Reading Program
- Professional indemnity insurance.

Those of us in practice at the time of these changes were only required to apply for a practising certificate and produce evidence of professional indemnity insurance.

Publicity-Press

Having sought permission of the President of the Bar Association, W B Campbell QC, for a ruling in relation to press interviews I was given permission to conduct one interview with the press and one interview on radio. I was asked not to be photographed for press or television in my wig and gown. I recall being following around by the press for the first couple of weeks and certainly having them attend most public functions which I attended for a long time thereafter. As time progressed I was invited by the press to comment on all sorts of public situations, many with which I declined to become involved after having been quoted as saying in one article that I would like to have become "a professional waterer of gardens". It is not an expression that rolls easily off my tongue even today. It did not take long to appreciate that much of what was reported in quotes in the newspapers was not in fact quoted material. On one occasion I was asked to be the week's racing tipster for an item headed *The Ladies' Choice*. Knowing nothing about horse racing (translated in the newspaper as "doesn't follow the horses often") someone at the *Courier Mail* made choices for me. I was glad I did not have a fling on Bellair at 4 to 1. Under the heading *Big wigs or faded germaniums?*, on the topic of wearing wigs and gowns in court, in the *Sunday Mail* of 27 July, 1969, there appears this entry: "One lady barrister, Miss N. J. Haxton, played safe by being witness for both the prosecution and the defence. 'I'd like to see the wig go because it flattens my hair' she said. 'But the robe is quite comfortable and I think some form of ceremonial dress has a place in the Supreme Court. We need something, a precedent, some differential to put people on their mettle'." Snippets of my address at the Somerville House speech night were headlined as "Girls urged to consider jobs". A forewarning of a debate conducted by the Portia Club read: "Next Tuesday night Queensland's first woman barrister, Miss Naida Haxton, will try to convince an audience that the emancipation of women was a mistake". There were advance notices of occasions on which I was to attend functions to speak, one topic being *A Woman In A Man's World* at the Australian Institute of Management, and one at a seminar held at Southport by South Coast women's organisations on the topic of *Abortion*.

One became, therefore, very cautious where the press were concerned and I gave up collecting cuttings.

Welcome from the Bar

On my first morning I was greeted with a huge bunch of flowers from the members of the Bar — an unexpected delight which served to make me feel quite welcome. At lunchtime I was approached by one of the members of my Chambers and asked: "Are you coming to the dining room? We're going down now". I was escorted past the formidable sign at the Common Room door which said "Members Only", treated as a member and graciously left to pay for what I ate and leave when I pleased. Whilst I was certainly a curiosity and many found my presence somewhat difficult to cope with, throughout my time at the Queensland Bar I was treated graciously, courteously, and considerately by nearly every member of the Judiciary and the Bar. I was made to feel welcome, I was treated as equally as it was possible to treat somebody equally in 1966 and I was expected to respond and to contribute on an equal footing. There were many minor incidents which, if taken out of context, may appear to be damning, but they were so few and far between that they made little impact upon the interesting experience of being the first and only woman to practice with around 100 men.

One very early comment which I recorded in my diary in May of 1967 is one I always found difficult to forget: "Outwardly we are being very nice to you, but inwardly we are bitterly resenting your presence". My greatest problem still is wondering whether the comment was made in jest, in seriousness, or just to show how clever the speaker was.

Chambers

Having acquired the Chambers of Bernard Goldberger together with the furniture therein, I added a mirror and a rocking chair. I still have the mirror which features in my 2005 portrait — *Looking Back on Looking Forward* — painted by Katerina Sakkas. These two items became over time the most used and visited parts of my Chambers by other members of the Bar. I also invested in a collection of vases as flowers seemed to be something which came from the profession, the solicitors and clients.

Briefs — Court Appearances

When I arrived in Chambers on my first day a brief to appear in court on an undefended divorce matter had been delivered. The solicitor, whose name I cannot recall and have not recorded, had delivered the brief shortly after my admission. It was his intention to be the first solicitor to brief the first practising woman barrister. At the same time I received a letter from the Office of the Minister for Justice and Attorney-General (Peter Delamothe, OBE), which stated:

> "I read with interest and pleasure of your admission to the Bar and of your intention to commence practice in Queensland.
>
> I write you this letter to offer my hearty congratulations and best wishes for your success.
>
> The report mentions that women have attained eminence at the Bar in many other parts of the world. I hope that you will be the first Queenslander to gain this enviable distinction.
>
> I shall be happy to give you a personal welcome if you would care to call on me. My private secretary will be pleased to make an appointment on hearing from you.
>
> I shall arrange for the Solicitor-General to be present."

That letter was followed up by a very prompt call to attend on the Attorney-General. At this meeting a brief was handed to me by the Solicitor-General. It was the wish of the Attorney-General that his brief would be the first brief to the first practising female barrister. Unfortunately he had missed by a whisker.

First Appearance in the Supreme Court

My first brief in the Supreme Court was, according to the press, one in which I "made Queensland legal history today and ...appeared for a woman plaintiff in an undefended divorce action" before the Honourable Mr Justice Douglas. As this matter was in Chambers, I do not recall how or why the press had access but it was reported in the newspapers that His Honour's comments were: "Congratulations on your first appearance in court — you handled it very well".

Other Early Briefs

I am no longer sure what my first appearance in any Court was but I suspect it was a matter in the Magistrates Court in which a taxi driver had been charged with "soliciting" passengers during a transport strike. I recall appearing against Graham Bell and taking in support of my submissions a copy of the *Oxford English Dictionary*. My argument was that the statement "anybody else for Mt Gravatt" said only once could not amount to soliciting. In the event I was successful. Some years later Graham Bell remembered that occasion and said to me: "I came into Court and saw this pretty little thing and decided this was going to be a walkover, and then you opened your mouth, you bitch".

One of my first cases was against David Jackson in a motor vehicle collision case in the Magistrates Court regarding liability. I recall submitting, at the end of the evidence, that it was more probable than not that either party could have been responsible for the accident and promptly lost that case. David very kindly gave me directions on more appropriate submissions to be made when addressing the court on future occasions in such cases.

Another case, of which there seemed to be many at the time, involved an accident with trams on a brief from the City Council's solicitor. After a full day including conferences and evidence in the Magistrates Court, one of my witnesses was asked in cross-examination a question to which his response was: "I'm sorry I can't answer that question". When asked by the magistrate: "Why not?, his response was: "It might bust me mate's story". An honest witness?

I recall another case of which others have since reminded me in which, once again in a motor vehicle negligence accident, appearing before a magistrate in Brisbane, the magistrate apportioned liability and awarded damages against a witness!

Early in my first year I appeared for a road sweeper in his 60s employed by the City Council. I think it was a maintenance matter. He appeared on the day of hearing in his best suit with a lace handkerchief in his pocket. The decision was reserved. The instructing solicitor subsequently rang me rather amused at a request from the client to pop up and tell the magistrate some thought that had just occurred to him. How difficult could we make the obtaining of justice if that were permitted?

In November 1967 I have noted in my diary that I received my first junior brief and did my first full Supreme Court matter in which, having succeeded, I obtained costs for my client.

In 1969 I received my first junior brief in the High Court to be heard in Brisbane. This was a property law matter in which I was led by Audley Gillespie-Jones whose poor eyesight required everything be read to him. I certainly knew every inch of that brief before we got to court.

I suspect every lawyer has interesting or unusual cases and clients but most disappear into the woodwork when the next brief appears. Some become gossip worthy at the time, some may grow into history. It is the layman who always wants the interesting bits.

It must have had something to do with my love of mathematics and theorems. I learned very early in practice to treat cases as though they were mathematical problems involving a given set of facts and an outcome or conclusion to be achieved by applying a known theorem, formula or equation to those given facts. So, having established what the problem was and the area of law in which it fell, I would set about making a list of what was needed to be proved and what was required to achieve it. This then formed the basis for any advices on evidence that might be required. I never changed this methodology and introduced a number of practitioners at the NSW Bar to it. In response to a question from a student in a property law class as to how to deal with a problem question, I once explained that system as a method for approaching those assignments. The apparent dearth of the use of advices on evidence is to be regretted: it saved time both in and out of court and saved costs if well done.

The diaries which I have retained show that I was in Court on average three days per week. On some days I have listed a number of matters which, on recollection, were what were called Chamber days on which, for example, undefended divorces, bankruptcy applications, probate applications and like matters were dealt with in Chambers by the Chamber Judge. Usually these applications challenged one's legal knowledge. On chamber matters Francis Douglas QC later had this to say in an article for the 2006 Winter Edition of *Bar News, The Journal of the NSW Bar Association*, on my retirement (at 68):

> "As an associate on the Queensland Supreme Court during the time that Naida was in busy practice, I had the opportunity to see her in action quite frequently. Prominent young practitioners against whom she appeared included David Jackson, Ian Gzell, Tony Fitzgerald, Ian Callinan, Geoff Davies, Bill Pincus and Bruce McPherson. It was a time of renewal at the Queensland Bar and even at that time, one perceived that these young practitioners as a group would ultimately have a profound influence upon the practice of law in Queensland.
>
> Naida appeared on a number of occasions in chambers before my father when I was his associate. It is not possible to adequately describe the intimacy of chambers practice during the late 1960's. The old Supreme Court building having been burnt down, the judges had no court rooms for civil work and conducted most of it in their chambers in rented accommodation. A chambers practice became precisely that. Naida did a wide range of work including, motions and summons in equity, common law and commercial matters and some matrimonial work which was then handled by the Supreme Court. She had good knowledge of Land Law having lectured at the University in this subject, as well as Commercial Law on which she lectured in the Department of Accountancy."

Other matters recorded in the early years were held in Magistrates Courts both in and out of Brisbane. I appeared at Ipswich, where I once had a police escort to leave the city after the defendant in my case had threatened to kill me for getting orders in favour of my client who was the plaintiff. Other locations included Landsborough, Beenleigh, Wynnum and Nambour where what should have been a one day case with Des Draydon for the opposition ran over and necessitated a rush to Woolworths for overnight essentials. Both of our instructing solicitors were well known to each of us but took it into their hands to ensure that our overnight arrangements should be gossip free by putting us up separately.

There were times when the briefs did not flow (as there are prone to be in barristers' practices) and I discovered amongst my papers this letter to a friend written on one of those occasions at the end of 1966:

Thursday 10:15 am

Dear Jan
I'm waiting for the telephone to ring!
I think I should make up a song to sing
One that tells of the time spent waiting and hoping
That something will happen — then moping
Because nothing seems to happen anymore
There is work about, work galore
But nobody loves me anymore — anymore!!

I thought they did, they seemed so nice
In finding me some crime and vice
But now you see they think I've had my fling
And here I am with nought to do but sing
I don't mind work and over books I'll eagerly pore
But what really makes me sore
Is that nobody loves me anymore — anymore!!

For four whole days I've sat and waited
For someone to make me feel feted.
At books on evidence and trusts I've glanced
And anything else on which my eyes have chanced.
South of Granada - something of a bore
Mitsui by Collette and nothing to do with law
You see nobody loves me anymore — anymore!!

So on I sit with boredom by my side
And my seat getting ever so wide
All about is a hive of activity and work
While I retreat a little further into the murk
And gloom of self-pity. Not one chore.
Is it any wonder I'm becoming a bore
Cos nobody loves me anymore — anymore!!

There were those who said — a seven-day wonder
It won't be long before she's thrown asunder
I laughed at them then — for I foolishly thought
A lady barrister is wanted and needed in court.
It seems they were right — the law
Is no place for a lady to soar,
Because nobody loves her anymore — anymore!!

They are paying me off, I know they are
The cheques are coming in from near and far.
But not a note, not a message saying are you free
On the ninth or the tenth to look after a client for
me.
I need meat and drink so I can't ignore
And Ethics forbid that I should implore
What a mess — and nobody loves me anymore —
anymore!!

So here I sit with nothing to do but dribble out
trash to the likes of you.
Please don't feel sorry and whatever you do, don't
ring
For you may prevent someone who hasn't a thing
About ladies-in-law
(If such there be)
From contacting me.
There must be somebody you see
Who really does love me!
N

Robing

At the time of my admission there was a Bar Robing Room at the Supreme Court. A locker was made available for me in the robing room, my name was attached to it and, on the first occasion that I was required to robe in the Supreme Court, one of the members of my Chambers ensured that I was escorted to the robing room and introduced to the vagaries and limitations of that place. As I had planned to, and did in fact, dress in Chambers and needed only to add wig, robe and bib at the Supreme Court, there did not appear to be any problem. Several weeks after I was admitted

I received a phone call from the Associate to the Chief Justice, Mack CJ, who informed me:

> "The Chief Justice has instructed me to inform you that on occasions when you need to robe at the Supreme Court he has arranged for you to have access to a room usually used by the jury and has made facilities available for you therein."

Apparently it was inappropriate for me to share a robing room with other members of my profession but not inappropriate for me to share a room with members of the jury. The reason for the phone call it later transpired was a report to the Chief Justice that I had been in the robing room and had seen a barrister "shirtless and in his singlet" and this could not be allowed to happen again. Having grown up in a family of males frequently seen shirtless or in their singlets, I might have considered the comment out of place except that there was an underlying impression that because I was a rarity in their midst most members of the profession were anxious to make me feel welcome and comfortable. There was quiet recognition around the legal profession that it was important that women take up practice at the Bar in Queensland. As the matter appeared to me to be more solicitude for my comfort I did, in fact, use the jury room as a robing room. When plans were put in place by the Justice Department for a new court building, the architect was sent to interview me in terms of what should be incorporated in a robing room for women barristers. When the new District Courts' building was opened in April 1970 it contained a very spacious and well fitted robing room for women at the Bar with the facilities that I had suggested as appropriate. Today it has become the acceptable practice for both male and female barristers to be seen in full robes in the street and robing rooms are hopefully less of a problem.

Bar Functions

There were a number of functions involving members of the Bar to which I was invited and at which I was made to feel very welcome, including a District Court Judge's party which was held towards the end of each year, the Bar Dinner which was held in May of most years when the High Court visited Brisbane for its annual sittings and Dining in Nights which were held in the Bar Association Common Room. Many of these functions were held at the Tattersalls Club or the United Services Club and, on many occasions, I recall being escorted into the premises through the side or back doors because women were not allowed on the premises. I have some diary notes from the first Bench and Bar Dinner held in June 1967 from which I have gleaned the following material.

Members of my floor had arranged discreetly that one of them would escort me to the function. I recall arriving and being greeted in a very welcoming manner. Garfield Barwick was then Chief Justice of the High Court and I was immediately introduced to him and the other members of the Court. My notes record "the food was exceptionally good for one of these dos and the wines quite superb. A dozen oysters, poached salmon steaks, veal mignon, apple slice with philly cheese and cream and Welsh rarebit with the port. Walter Campbell made a toast to the Queen. Many people came visiting our table. Campbell then made the first speech of the evening welcoming the visitors and announcing what an historic occasion it was that I should be the first woman ever to have graced their dinner with her presence. Sir Garfield Barwick replied to the Mr Junior speech and addressed the gathering: 'Mr Chairman, my brethren, etc, and my fair lady to whom I shall come back later' … After dinner we adjourned outside where those who had not previously met me made a point of doing so … a most delightful evening". As was to become another considered and thoughtful habit, a member of the Bar would ensure that I was escorted from the function to a taxi so as not to be embarrassed in any way. Gerry Brennan QC was always ready to offer his services in this regard.

Lecturing

Before the end of my first year at the Bar I was invited by Dr Tarlo, who was Dean of the Law School at Queensland University, to undertake his Land Law lectures. Dr Tarlo had taken on the position on the death of Walter Harrison and was finding the load of administrative work associated with being Dean of the Faculty made it very difficult for him to give the lectures. I was formally appointed to the "part-time staff at the university as a Part-Time Lecturer in Land Law in the Department of Law" at a remuneration of $10 per lecture. For a period of about four months, on Mondays, I juggled briefs and two sets of lectures to day students and evening students. I recall two of my students who both obtained, to the best of my recollection, High Distinctions, being Francis Douglas now F M Douglas QC of the NSW Bar and Paul Finn, subsequently Professor at ANU and Justice Finn of the Federal Court. Following the apparent success of this lecturing appointment I was invited by the Commerce Faculty to lecture in Commercial Law which I did to a combined group of day and evening students late enough in the day to avoid complications with Court appearances. It was a time of many protest demonstrations on campus and often erratic attendances. I recall that the commerce students were always keen to invite me to their social events. This was the first time I became involved in setting and marking exam papers. Marking was the interesting exercise. Marking seemed an endless task in which I recognised early in the piece what an interesting impact the readability of handwriting could have on the need to assess the answers fairly. On one occasion I was amused by a female student who had apparently spent the three hours transcribing the problem questions on the paper into capital letters and shorthand, which was confirmed to be perfect shorthand. One of the questions asked for "explanatory" notes on the following … to which the response was to make up 73 words from the word "explanatory".

Law Reporting

In 1968, I was interviewed by the Incorporated Council of Law Reporting for the State of Queensland in relation to a position as a reporter on the Queensland Reports (Qd R). I recall Fairleigh QC asking me what would happen if I got married and left the Bar to have children (an interesting assumption in retrospect) and my replying that I thought it (law reporting) was probably the very thing one could do from home in such an eventuality. The subsequent emphasis on law reporting in later years was perhaps vindication although not undertaken for the reason suggested. I was merely a reporter in training when I left the Queensland Bar.

Public Functions

As the first woman practising barrister I was frequently invited to attend public functions either as guest speaker or in some other capacity. I was invited to become the Convenor for Laws and the Legal Position of Women on the National Council of Women of Queensland and filled that position for a number of years. I took up a similar role in NSW. I continued to take an active part in Queensland Debating Union Interstate Grade Championships and acted as an adjudicator for the Queensland Debating Union. I was, for a number of years, a Committee Member of the Women Graduates Association and a speaker at many of their functions. Some of the groups to which I spoke included the National Council of Women, the Women Graduates Association, Law School students, Queensland University students, Portia Club and numerous other women's organisations. Some of the topics upon which I gave speeches were very topical at the time — the 1960s being the era in which rights were on top of the agenda. Topics on which I spoke included the following:

- A Woman in a Man's World
- Free and equal to what
- Recognition of the Responsibilities of Equality
- The rights of women — legal and civil
- Abortion Law Reform
- The right to die
- Diminishing rights of the individual
- Freedom and Equality

Other activities with which I became involved included:

- By invitation of the Attorney-General, Visitor to the women's gaol in Brisbane.
- Judge at the Student of the Year Quest for Quota Club
- Participating in an annual careers night organised by the Women Graduates.
- By invitation of the Chief Justice of the High Court, a member of the Australian Conservation Foundation Legal Subcommittee, which involved keeping up with legislation in the areas of local government and environmental law and reporting to the Foundation.
- In consultation with Margaret Kelly, solicitor, and others, organised the female members of the profession in Brisbane to host a luncheon at the 1969 Australian Legal Convention. This luncheon was held at the United Services Club Ladies Annex and attended by about 16-20 women, including Roma Mitchell from South Australia, Elizabeth Hart, Alayne Peterson, Margaret Kelly, Jean Russell and others. There was no such thing as a women lawyers' association. As the "senior" member of the women who were lawyers — barristers being senior to solicitors — it apparently behoved me to play the part.

Other Recalled Incidents, Attitudes and Gossip

At the end of my first year at the Bar I have noted that on appearances before Justice Hanger he persisted in calling me "Mr Haxton". In subsequent years I received correspondence addressed to N J Haxton Esq. I did not know what to think so resorted to my favourite source of information, my encyclopaedic dictionary, where I discovered that Esquire is "a title of dignity next in line to a knight. It is properly given to … barristers-at-law

... indeed in ordinary usage treated as a mere complimentary adjunct to a person's name in the addresses of letters, in which case it is abbreviated to Esq". I decided it should be taken as a compliment acknowledging my status and not contemplate taking offence.

In connection with the many occasions on which I was asked to give talks on "rights" my fellow barristers took to calling me "Naida Indira Pankhurst".

When I first arrived at the Inns of Court the washrooms were labelled "Members" and "Staff" which reflected the gender of the then members and staff. For some time it was a facetious topic of conversation as to whether or not I should be required to use the Members' washroom.

I was often invited to parties and dinners and occasions to which I would not have been invited as an ordinary member of the Bar. These included a dinner for Lord Denning to whom I was introduced and with whom I conversed for some considerable time. I then spent quite a while talking to Lady Denning mainly about their daughter who was a barrister and the daughter's troubles with au pair girls. On another occasion I was invited to go bushwalking with a visiting Law Lord and to be present at some meeting place on a mountain west of Brisbane with a baked damper in time for morning tea. I recall that Bruce McPherson (later McPherson JA) was in charge of the fire for the billy tea.

Following the fire in the old Supreme Court building in September 1968, I was deputed to help organise unoccupied members of the Bar to give time to rescuing the water-damaged books from the Supreme Court Library. The books had been removed to large warehouse-like premises at the end of Roma Street where they were placed on trestles and fanned by huge fans. It was the task of members of the Bar and other volunteers to turn the pages as delicately as possible whenever they might have some free time. This rescue operation took some considerable time and organisation. Graham Bell and I found ourselves on more than one of these voluntary exercises and, when I queried why we seemed always to get them, his rationale was that because we were single we had more spare time for these kinds of exercises.

In 1970, I was formally invited to the Official Opening of the District Courts Building by Her Majesty the Queen. Following the opening we went to the basement of the new building to meet the Queen. Conversation was very short and uninteresting. It seemed a very strange place to have her meet people when there was a whole new building available. The ceiling was concrete covered in pipes. I recall thinking how small she was and what tiny feet she had.

In 1970, I also organised a series of lectures on women and the law for the YWCA and was invited to join the United Nations Human Rights Legal Sub-Committee for Queensland. There was certainly plenty to do.

For nearly a year from August 1967, I kept a diary of things happening around me in practice. It provides a number of comments on various occasions from fellow members of the Bar and from students whom I lectured at the university including, in 1967: "everyone is still so overawed by your presence, so much so, that they can only admire you". In that year also I was asked to talk to law students at the University of Queensland on the topic, *Being a Woman Barrister*. As I was not entirely sure what this topic meant and had little time to prepare, I rushed around Chambers after court asking the following questions:

1. What do you think of women at the Bar?
2. Why do you think that?
3. Do you think there should be more of them?
4. Do you see any particular advantages or disadvantages?

I have transcribed the following from the original handwritten notes still in my possession and from which I constructed a talk on the run.

> "I wish she wasn't here. I'd get some more work.
> Don't make any difference; it just makes it difficult to swear at times.
> It saves going outside for sex.
> Most people here like it — it's different.
> Six would be highly desirable.
> More divergent opinions could make a difference.
> Think about being a barrister not a lady barrister.
> No professional organisation.
> Should have more of you.
> Oh! Hell! Think it's marvellous. Should be more of them. Two qualifications — good looking and not cleverer than I am.
> I think it's lovely.
> Alright — women who shouldn't be frightened of being accepted.
> They've got some disadvantages:
> 1. Their voices can be too thin.
> 2. Males prefer to have men appearing for them.

3. Outside court, female litigants feel as if they have a better deal from men.

Don't like em. And ladies shouldn't be involved in tendentious arguments in public places.
I heartily approve. If there are no women at the Bar the experiences of 50 per cent of the population are not brought to bear on solution to problems.
Disadvantages — Victorian embarrassments with women.
No comment.
No way.
It will depend on what they looked like.
The Bar is not the place for women — it's a little unfeminine.
I think it is an excellent idea provided they have certain qualities of mental toughness which you possess and which doesn't necessarily flow from academic distinction.
A good thing. Should be more of them. Sort of profession that there is no reason why shouldn't have women in it as well as men. What does concern me is where work is likely to come from.
Damn good idea. Like the company of women. Disadvantages — none.
Great idea. Can't see any difference. Not exclusive province of mine.
Very good thing:

1. Such an insular profession anything to broaden the scope would be desirable to start with.
2. Evidence — the cases are heard by men, some clients have invincible repugnance to talking to men.
3. Don't know anything about the Children's Court. Women may be effective.
4. Bar for women could be a stepping stone to Children's Court and domestic cases.

Treated the same as everyone else but there will be:

1. Barristers who don't like women;
2. Solicitors who don't like women;
3. Clients themselves who don't like women;
4. Some judges who don't like women.

Loverly (sic). Women in any profession moderate things and put men on better behaviour and sharpen the competitive element for men to conduct themselves better. I don't see any disadvantage — trend towards equality.

Don't like it but purely a prejudice. Think if they want to come they should be given a fair shot. Major disadvantage — prejudice.

Think it's a good idea — would welcome more — women have their part to play. Can't see any disadvantages. Masculine society has become very narrow and women have a fresh viewpoint.

I think of them all the time. You have convinced me that women can be successful.

Main disadvantage is an out-of-court one — from solicitors and embarrassed clients. There may be an advantage with some of the judges.

A great asset — why — because of their devious minds. Disadvantages are in moments of embarrassment.

They're all right. Better than men. Not enough of them.

The Disadvantages:

1. Something new in law
2. Criminal cases — feeling of unease among jury
3. No disadvantages in most civil cases
4. Socially

Good idea if competent and want to — disadvantages none."

How interesting it would be to conduct the same experiment today.

At some time, not recollected, I became the official scorer for the barristers v solicitors annual cricket match and once had a token bat as twelfth man on the Gabba in one of those games.

Overall Impressions

As to practice itself: When I joined the Queensland Bar in 1966 I was 24, I was young, raw, stitched-up, naïve and, on occasion, an embarrassment. I think I left the Queensland Bar a lot more mature, a lot more experienced, more street wise (thanks in no small part to Des Draydon, a former police officer, who took it upon himself to ensure that I became "street wise" and would insist on taking me on excursions to acquire background for specific briefs) and a lot less stressed probably at the end of each day. I firmly believed (and continue to believe) that I was admitted as a "barrister" not as "female barrister" or a "woman barrister". This was one reason that I never joined a women lawyers association. I considered that the professional body for members of the Bar, the Bar Association, was there to serve all barristers and expected it to do so. I would have been happy to join, for example, a Property Lawyers Association, for it would have been useful in practice. I read recently with interest the 2015 *barnews* (The Journal of the NSW Bar Association) featuring the topic of parental responsibilities and the Bar and the issues which parenthood brings to the work role of all barristers, whether male or female. At last the discussion is out in the open for all barristers, whereas, 40-50 years ago, whether women had children and how they were cared for was kept very close as it might impact on the receipt of work. Mind you childcare or childminding was then somewhere between non-existent and primitive. If there were occasions on which I was unwelcome or disadvantaged they were very minor in comparison to the positive, honest and welcoming manner in which the Queensland Bar accepted my presence. Many of the experiences and friendships which I treasure derive from my years at the Queensland Bar. It was a novel, exciting, interesting and, as I often said, "hysterical" time in my life.

As to the outcomes of practice, I once wrote in a letter to a legal friend, "Yesterday my poor little mother got back custody of her kids and as a result I have a beautiful potted African violet plus cuttings of a Cooktown Orchid and enough lilies to start a full-scale garden. It is nice to be thanked in such a different way, but it is also very sad. One never knows whether one has really done the best, but just that, in the circumstances that are made public, it is 'probably' the best. It is the dealing with all these probabilities that does tend perhaps to make one a little hardened, for to become involved in feelings (particularly those of other people) can be counterproductive". Experience grew confidence and confidence, dispassionateness.

Post Queensland

In 1971, I married David Harry Boddam-Whetham, a chemical engineer from Sydney, with three sons in their early teens in boarding school, and who himself had just begun 10 years with the New South Wales Government as Principal Gas Engineer and subsequently Adviser on Energy. I agreed to marry on the understanding that I would not change my name, as I was not "going to explain that name to every magistrate and judicial officer in the country". I felt reasonably confident that there was still a viable reputation attached to my single name. When, at the end of 1970, I told a senior member of the Queensland Bar what my plans were the response was: "Why would you want to do that? If you stay around here for another 15 years you will be on the Bench". I had not seen this as a realistic alternative at the time although David and I had investigated the possibility of living out of two homes. I did not and have not regretted the move to NSW.

Practice in NSW

In the meantime I accepted a place with the State Crown Solicitor's Office in Sydney in order to make myself familiar with New South Wales law and set about making plans for being admitted to the Bar in NSW. My husband knew Jeremy Badgery-Parker and I went and talked to Jeremy about finding chambers. There was a group of barristers in a very strange little outfit at 127 (I think it was) Phillip Street, Sydney, and I made plans to join them. In February 1972, I was admitted to the Bar of New South Wales as Naida Haxton and started practice there in Phillip Street getting briefs from people on the floor and around the place. Here was the nucleus for the start of the original Frederick Jordan Chambers. When Frederick Jordan Chambers opened up at 233 Macquarie Street I joined them there. As I was again required to spend 12 months as a pupil, Murray Tobias (later a Judge of the Court of Appeal) willingly took me on. This was a good connection because his clerk, Les O'Brien, was very helpful at getting me work. The NSW Bar worked quite differently to the Queensland Bar which, when I was there, did not use a clerking system.

I also found that the atmosphere in chambers was very different and to some degree a bit of a culture shock. One got briefs thrown at the last minute, which was something I had not experienced in Queensland in those days. Some of the young barristers would accept two or three briefs and then take the best one at the last minute and leave the others flying about to be taken by someone else and, if you accepted the brief, you would be left with having to work out whether you could actually deal with the matter or you needed an adjournment. I just found it was a slightly different culture of how one got work, how you were dealt with by the other people at the Bar. There were certainly a lot more people at the Bar. There was more competition, and of course my biggest disadvantage was being unknown in Sydney. Nobody had gone to school with me, to university with me, or practised with me or sent me work as a lawyer. So that was a hard one. Needless to say I found that people were very good. Bob St John was on my floor. Bob used to give me a lot of devilling work. I used to do a lot of draft opinions and writing and research for him. He would pay me promptly, which was absolutely wonderful. I did quite a bit of that for various people. That, I think, perhaps conveyed confidence that I did have skills.

One redeeming feature was, however, the presence of other women in practice so my appearances in court were not likely to be novel. I had joined the Queensland Bar as one woman on a Roll of 214 practitioners, approximately 110 of whom were in practice. I joined the NSW Bar when there were 560 males and 13 women on the Roll. I was already acquainted with Janet Coombs, Cecily Backhouse, Jane Mathews and Mary Gaudron. People talked to me about Beatrice Gray, who was overseas in the New Hebrides, later Vanuatu, at the time doing legal work, and they kept saying to me, "Oh you'll like her. You and she will get on together". When she did come back and joined us in Frederick Jordan Chambers, we did become quite good friends. We were later both pregnant at the same time and hell-bent on hiding it.

There were a couple of solicitors who briefed me quite a lot. One of them was Barbara Holborow, later to become a Children's Court Magistrate. There was one young solicitor, whose name I have completely forgotten, who used to get me to draft his standard documents for office use. I did quite a bit of that kind of work. People frequently asked: "What was the most memorable or most interesting case you were involved in?" It is not an easy question to answer. All cases were important in one sense. They certainly are to the client. The cases one remembers often have nothing to do with their relative legal importance. I did appear as a junior in 1972 in *The Attorney-General v Mundey* [1972] 2 NSWLR 887 which was a case involving contempt. While Jack Mundey was involved in many public demonstrations so were many students of the era involved in anti-Vietnam War activities that frequently ended in court. The profession around Australia was willing to do pro bono representations. I had one such brief and at the end of the pre-court conference with two concerned parents and the young male defendant, I inquired whether the beard on the young face had been present at the time. "It had not" was the answer. I quietly suggested to the instructing solicitor that when he arrived at court he should sit the young man with others at the back of the court but visible to the bench and the witness box. The prosecution started their evidence and when asked if they could identify the defendant in court could not and the magistrate dismissed the case without any need for the defendant to give evidence much to the delight of two anxious parents.

One difficult and very embarrassing case was when I accepted a junior brief to Bob St John in some dispute over building renovations at the Astor Apartment building and I had not had or been to a conference with the client. That was a pretty disastrous morning. Just after the civil jury were sworn he said: "Oh well, my defamation trial has been called. It's all yours. Here's the brief". The matter was before Justice Gordon Samuels who realised what was going on, but fortunately we were able to and did settle it. That was a little bit of the culture at the time.

One unforgettable appearance was in March 1974, some 10 or so days before son James was born, in a District Court building dispute matter, the first day I was "Miss Haxton"; the second day I was "Mrs Haxton"; the fourth day I stood up to address at the end of evidence, and the Judge said to me, "Mrs Haxton, would you like to sit down?" And I'm standing there with my hands on my tummy saying: "No, your Honour, it is much more comfortable standing up".

An unusual case was for breach of promise involving the successful return of a rather expensive diamond engagement ring. Breach of promise cases were rather rare and I suspect today nobody has ever heard of them, much less been involved in one.

Lecturing

Shortly after joining the Bar in Sydney, in 1973, I was appointed Tutor in Real Property for the Law Extension Committee of the University of Sydney and Senior Tutor from 1975-1979. From 1975-1979, I was Standby Examiner in Real Property for the Barristers and Solicitors Admission Boards. This work principally involved setting assignment topics and marking the responses. It also involved, as I believe it still does, lecturing at weekend schools. In 1978, I was for a short time a part time lecturer in Commercial Law in the Faculty of Business Studies at what was to become the UTS. When one of the lecturers was looking for a stand-in, while on leave, for his Commercial Law lectures for real estate students. I agreed, before being told I would also be required to give lectures in Communications to the same students and he did not have a curriculum. Where to start to learn? There always seems to be some book on the topic which provides an outline guide. And so I played games with sitting half the class facing the front and half the class facing the back and getting them to test the differences and getting them writing letters to 10 year olds, to gift givers for flowers when in hospital, writing ads for houses and land etc, etc. I suspect that I learned as much as the students did.

Whilst I was Assistant Editor and Editor of the *New South Wales Law Reports* (NSWLR) for the Council of Law Reporting for NSW between 1981 and 2006, I gave many lectures and seminars on law reporting, headnote writing and editing in Sydney and in other States of Australia and in New Zealand. I once gave a presentation on judgment writing to the Judges of the Land and Environment Court. I also lectured on law reporting and headnote writing in the NSW Bar Association Continuing Education Program.

Law Reporting — What is Law Reporting?

Law Reports are series of books often seen by the shelf load behind legal eagles on television and which contain judgments from a selection of decisions handed down by courts. In common law countries, including Australia, court opinions are legally binding under the rule of *stare decisis* or precedent. That rule requires a court to apply a previous legal principle that was established by a court of the same jurisdiction dealing with a similar set of facts. The regular publication of judgments establishing new principles or applying old principles in a new area of law is important so that everyone involved in legal work can find out what the law is as declared by judges. A law report is more than just the judgment. It begins with a headnote which includes the names of the parties, the date of the hearing and the names of the judge or judges, followed by catchwords, which are indexing terms locating the judgment in the relevant area of law, and then a summary of the facts and the principles of law applied as determined by the barrister or solicitor reporting the case. Those reporting the cases are called reporters and those selecting the cases from hundreds of published judgments and approving the headnotes for publication are called editors. A broad knowledge of the law and general principles are essential for the editor and reporter, though a reporter can concentrate on specialist areas of the law. An editor needs to be able to work out what should be reported, why it should be reported and how it should be reported. The law reports serve a principle of accountability in promoting equality before the law, reliance upon the system of precedent, exposure of judicial decision making to public scrutiny and efficiency in providing accessibility with relevance and usefulness. On the following page is an example of what a headnote looks like:

64 NSWLR 125] R v WILKIE 125

R v WILKIE and Others*
[2005] NSWCCA 311

Court of Criminal Appeal: Spigelman CJ, Ipp JA and Adams J

29 August 2005

Criminal Law — Practice and procedure — Prosecution — Commonwealth offence — Trial to be held "in the State" where offence committed — Audio visual evidence given outside State — Evidence not unconstitutional — Commonwealth of Australia Constitution Act 1900, s 80.

High Court and Federal Judiciary — Criminal jurisdiction and procedure — Trial by jury — Indictable offences — Trial to be held "in the State" where offence committed — Audio visual evidence given outside State — Evidence received within State — Evidence not unconstitutional — Commonwealth of Australia Constitution Act 1900, s 80.

The *Commonwealth of Australia Constitution Act* 1900, s 80, provides:

"**80 Trial by jury**

The trial on indictment of any offence against any law of the Commonwealth shall be by jury, and every such trial shall be held in the State where the offence was committed, and if the offence was not committed within any State the trial shall be held at such place or places as the Parliament prescribes."

Held: The taking of evidence by means of an audio visual link from a witness physically situate overseas does not contravene the *Commonwealth of Australia Constitution Act* 1900, s 80, when it provides that every "trial on indictment" for an offence against the law of the Commonwealth shall be held "in the State" where the offence was committed. (127 [5], 129 [21])

Decision of Howie J in *R v Wilkie, Burroughs, Mainprize* [2005] NSWSC 794, affirmed.

Note:
A Digest (3rd ed) — CRIMINAL LAW [689]; HIGH COURT AND FEDERAL COURT [201]

CASES CITED

The following cases are cited in the judgments:

Attorney-General (NSW) v Brewery Employés Union of NSW (1908) 6 CLR 469
Bell Group Ltd (In Liq) v Westpac Banking Corporation (2004) 208 ALR 491
Brown v The Queen (1986) 160 CLR 171
Brownlee v The Queen (2001) 207 CLR 278
Cheatle v The Queen (1993) 177 CLR 541
Director of Public Prosecutions v Alexander (1993) 33 NSWLR 482

* [EDITORIAL NOTE: An application for special leave to appeal to the High Court was refused.]

Papua New Guinea Law Reports — PNGLR

I had just started at the Bar in NSW, we'd just moved into the new chambers, so I was probably within my first six or eight months of practice in Sydney when (the) Law Book Co asked me would I edit the *Papua New Guinea Law Reports* (PNGLR) because they were allied to Queensland law, and somebody in Queensland had recommended that I might like to do it because I had already started doing some of that work in Queensland. That someone was the then Editor, Maxwell Morley, who had been a near neighbour in the Inns of Court in Brisbane. That was the start of my first editing job in the area of law reporting and lasted until 1992 when the Council of Law Reporting for Papua New Guinea decided to publish the reports themselves. As the work involved was actually putting together an annual volume which might contain 60 cases, most of which had been reported in PNG, it was something that could be done in quiet moments. Shortly after taking on the editing I was asked to do the reporting as well. Papua New Guinea became an Independent State in 1975, with a new and very modern Constitution. I thoroughly enjoyed the challenges involved in coming to grips with a new and exciting era for the country and especially in reporting the cases interpreting the Constitution undertaken by a Full Court of five judges, most of whom, in the early days, were from Australia or the UK. The late Sir Sidney Frost, as Chairman of the PNG Council, had given me fairly free rein to "polish" the judgments. He was followed by the late Sir William Prentice, Warwick Andrew who later sat on the NSW District Court and finally Sir Mari Kapi. With encouragement from a longstanding friend and supporter, the late Sir Harry Gibbs, I endeavoured to maintain a standard for those Reports which would ensure their prestige in the Pacific region. The time with PNG was some of the most interesting in terms of new law and new procedures for that emerging nation and certainly in terms of law reporting. Sir William Prentice came to Sydney in March 1974 to offer me a trip to PNG. He was somewhat surprised to find that Miss Haxton was very, very pregnant and the offer unfortunately was never renewed.

Digesting and Indexing

Law Book Co (later to become Thompson Reuters) who published the PNGLR, invited me to provide entries to the *Australian Legal Monthly Digest* (ALMD) in a format and style approved by the managing editor. The ALMD was at that time a paper only production. They started me on quantum of damages cases. Piles of unpublished judgments in negligence cases would arrive and were required to be condensed into bare essentials and indexed. It became a soul-destroying task which at one stage caused me to stop driving a car for nearly three months. I could not wait to pass it on. I then progressed to "digesting" cases from the local government and town planning areas across all States, the NSWLR and the *Local Government Reports of Australia* (LGRA) later the *Local Government and Environment Law Reports* (LGERA). What this did, however, was to provide me with a great working knowledge of the *Australian Digest* (A Digest) and its usefulness especially if entries were properly catchworded and indexed. When I became Assistant Editor of the NSWLR, then published by Law Book Co, I was asked if I would produce an index of the published volumes to that time, such an index never having been compiled. I was provided with a full set of the NSWLR and a full set of the A Digest. The task took some considerable time and occupied much space in the rumpus room at home for months, but it certainly increased my knowledge of the A Digest and the enormous value in consistency of indexing legal principles. As it was well before the days of computers all entries were dictated, then individually typed onto A5 paper perforated to card size, the entries then separated and shuffled. As there was little consistency in either the NSWLR catchwords or the A Digest entries of those cases, it involved a lot of rewriting and reshuffling but it did provide a workable basis for future additions. By the time I retired from the Bar in 2006, I had edited various editions of the *NSWLR Consolidated Tables and Indices* from 1971 to 2005 and had become very conversant with the ease of production that was occasioned by the advent of digital printing. When the NSWLR became self-publishing at the end of the 1990s, the Index and Tables became a regular part of the production of the Reports. Later I was able to guide Beatrice Gray in the production of a similar Index for the *State Reports (New South Wales)*, (SR (NSW). I admit to being a strong advocate to the Consultative Council of Law Reporting and the Australian Institute of Judicial Administration for the adoption, Australian wide, of such a system of indexing for reports and judgments.

New South Wales Law Reports — NSWLR

I came to NSWLR in my tenth year of editing the PNGLR. I was invited to an interview with Joe Bannon QC, the then Chair of the Council of Law Reporting for NSW, and Dyson Heydon, recently appointed Editor of the NSWLR. I was asked to become Assistant Editor of the NSWLR because my work on the PNGLR had been noticed and was recognised: "We have looked at your work on PNGLR and like what you are doing". The Council was then funded out of a "bottom drawer" at the Attorney-General's Department and housed in the Chief Secretary's Building in Bridge Street in Sydney. "What we will offer you is: you can use the Council's chambers as yours and you will provide assistance to Dyson Heydon as the editor." The office was staffed by Enid Hartnett who had come from the Attorney-General's Department and was the backbone of the office. Enid served with great skill and attention to detail for 16 years. I was subsequently asked to act as Honorary Secretary to the Council of Law Reporting. Little did I know that it would take over my legal career and how entrepreneurial I would become?

The Council of Law Reporting and its advisors

For over 26 years I worked with a number of Councils. Joe Bannon, QC, was my first Chairman. In his day the Council met in the Bar Association Board Room: he did all the correspondence and personally shouted the members a drink at the end of each year. His interest in copyright proved invaluable to the Council and its continuing publication. Win Howard, Solicitor, and Garry Downes, QC, who followed in succession, both ensured the electronic rights in a version of the NSWLR, given away by the Attorney-General of the day, without consultation, were retrieved and protected. Downes and I spent the best part of one vacation preparing for litigation, which, thankfully, was settled. At this time Charles Alexander at Minter Ellison became the Council's first solicitor and later introduced Margaret Calvert, from Ebsworths, Solicitors, when he found himself with a conflict of interest. I talked to Margaret about an idea for one source for both print and electronic production of the Reports after data had ended up in ownership of Butterworths and print source in ownership of the Council. Margaret introduced me to Peter Meyer who was then at Desktop Law. He knew what I was talking about when I said we must be able to go electronic from print, or vice versa, and who used his legal background as well as his IT knowledge to help produce the digital version of NSWLR. Margaret guided the Council through the tender contracts, service agreements and came up with a one-page licensing agreement at the end of the process. Peter, introduced by Margaret as someone who might know what to do, proved capable of explaining to mystified Council members the logic of Standard Generalised Mark-up Language (SGML), then guided the Council through policy, strategy, planning, world-wide tendering, evaluation of tenders and project supervision and management.

The project would never have happened without him and the attention to detail shown by his staff. The Attorney-General gave his full support. Francis Douglas, QC, grasped what we were all talking about and ensured that the Council made a decision to become self-publishing and to recapture an authorised version of the NSWLR; Joe Campbell, QC, persisted in making sure all of the page ends and line breaks were honoured on the electronic version of the Reports. Dr Chris Birch, SC, helped to ensure that *Dowling's Select Cases*, edited by a Council member, lived to see the light of day and for encouraging the production of an index to the SR(NSW) which were the precursor to the NSWLR.

As Honorary Secretary to the Council, I became responsible for preparing the monthly meetings of the Council including all agendas and papers. Council meetings dealt with a huge range of matters including those relating to production of the Reports and Indices, financial management, office management and salaries, possible new projects, relationships with service providers and licensees and copyright matters.

Justice Heydon, AC, who had attended Council meetings while Editor, had this to say on my retirement:

> "In Council meetings, or other meetings, or debates, she was a formidable antagonist. She agreed with Dr Johnson's dictum that 'to treat your adversary with respect is to give him an advantage to which he is not entitled'. Her attitude to decision-making in committees was similar to that of A D Lindsay, who when Master of Balliol College Oxford, on finding himself in a minority of one, said: 'I see we are deadlocked'. All through the last 26 years she has shown the qualities which Lord Carrington noticed in Margaret Thatcher. When asked: 'What will happen if Margaret Thatcher is run over by a bus?' Lord Carrington replied: 'It wouldn't dare'. By her labours, and her ruthless control of costs, she made the New South Wales Law Reports the cheapest set of law reports in the country, apart from one other series probably the fastest, and, I would suggest, the most accurate."

The Editor

I only knew one Editor in my time on the NSWLR. For nearly 20 years I was Assistant Editor to J D Heydon, Barrister. I think we understood each other from day one. He knew and understood what the Reports were about and how they should communicate to the users. In the whole of the time that we worked together, I recall only a handful of conversations that lasted longer than a minute or two. More often than not a cryptic noted passed to and fro. By way of example, he forbade me from using his postnominals on the reports. The correspondence goes like this:

> *Kirby P to Haxton*: The front cover of the New South Wales Law Reports indicates that Mr J.D. Heydon is Editor. Mr Heydon's postnominals (sic) "QC" are omitted. This betokens an excess of modesty .... Could I suggest that the QC be added ....
> *Haxton to Heydon:* ... I am putting you as J D Heydon QC from the beginning of Volume 13.
> *Heydon to Haxton:* I forbid it.
> *Haxton to Heydon:* Please explain to me why? "Heydon forbids it" is a funny answer to give to the increasing number of inquiries! ... Hardwicke is beside himself at the thought that I continue to describe you as a "mere" barrister.
> *Heydon to Haxton: ... Indeed!!!!*
> *Haxton to Kirby P (drafted by Heydon):* ... The Editorial functions in respect of NSWLR are controlled by the Council and have been since March 1963. It was (and is) an editorial decision not to add Mr Heydon's postnominals. ...

When a pile of judgments would be sent to Heydon to decide on reportability they came back marked on the front — R (reportable), NR (not reportable), or HPA (hold pending appeal): headnotes for approval to go to the printer were marked HNOK (headnote OK). It was such an efficient use of time that I continued it when Editor. Very occasionally there might be a brief comment such as a suggestion to report certain portions only of the judgment. I was left to make the relevant excision and to account for its deletion by inserting a summary or a note that said something like "His Honour then considered matters not calling for report". James Merralls, AO, QC as Editor of the *Commonwealth Law Reports* (CLR) was accustomed to refer to this as "Naida's filleting".

Despite the brevity of our communications we developed an unspoken rapport and understanding which I greatly appreciated and that I am sure benefited the Reports.

The Reporters

Many of the reporters stayed around almost as long as I did. I think that Ron Desiatnik and I both started as reporters in 1972. Beatrice Gray, Camilla Sakkas, Michael Barr and Ian Newbrun joined us in the 1980s. Richard Scruby, one of the research assistants, took up the task when admitted to the Bar. They all, at various times, expressed to me their addiction to the discipline of reporting.

Assistants and verifiers or research assistants

Before publication the judgments go through a process of checking quotes and citations of cases and statutes and styling which we called verification. I was blessed over the years to have very loyal and committed staff. When I started in the position Enid Hartnet ran the office, did the verifying and did the work of what later became the positions of the Production Manager and Editorial Assistant. She was later assisted by Liz Watt. When Enid retired, Kath Rosic took over for a couple of years and returned as part-time Office Manager some years later. At one stage in the mid-1990s the PA was Stephen Sheehan with terrific word processing skills. There were always a number of people in the background whose jobs were to ensure that the production happened as and when and how it should. Hella Ochocki at the publisher, Law Book Co, had major input into the form and delivery of the final production for many years. Michelle Ikin started two days per week as a PA when her son started school and ended up as a full-time production assistant by the time he was in high school. Michelle's attention to detail and daily emphasis on reprioritising work flows were invaluable. At this time also, I started using university students, many of whom were friends of son James, for verification or research work. They proved to be a multi-skilled lot, who enjoyed the task and especially the access to libraries such as the Supreme Court Library, the Bar Association Library and on the odd occasion the Mitchell Library.

Mary Maher, with a BA/LLB from Sydney, left to start work as a solicitor at Baker & McKenzie, Sydney, and then moved to their Chicago office, where she acquired an LLM International and an LLM in Taxation from the University of Chicago Law School. She then began work with the LLM programs at Northwestern University School of Law as the Associate Director of Legal Careers. Northwestern recently received a much publicised huge donation ($100 mil) from the Pritzker family and is now known as the Northwestern Pritzker School of Law.

Paul Salisbury picked up not one, but two, University Medals from Sydney, was conversant in many Asian and European languages and when last heard of was working at the Australian Embassy in Tokyo. "I basically work as an advisor and analyst on international trade negotiations, including bilateral trade negotiations (FTAs) and regional negotiations like the Trans Pacific Partnership (TPP). I also worked on Australia's whaling case against Japan at the International Court of Justice in The Hague" he emailed me after receiving an OAM for services to the international community following the earthquakes and tsunami which occurred in Japan in 2011. Paul was a great help in plotting the logistics of the data conversion processes.

Katie Wrigley and Clarissa Amato took over the running of the office and job shared very efficiently when the then PA suddenly left. Katie Wrigley, who became a solicitor, is currently Principal Solicitor at the Refugee Advice and Casework Service Inc [RACS] in Sydney. She has recently been involved with the Bar Association in setting up a Refugee Justice Network to facilitate smooth referrals for judicial review. She has also been mentoring lawyers from a range of cultural backgrounds, including those from former torture and from torture backgrounds. Katie herself was a finalist for the Women in Law Mentor of the Year award. RACS was a finalist for a number of awards in 2015 including the Lawyers' Weekly Boutique Diversity Law Firm of the Year and the Human Rights Commission's Human Rights Awards. Clarissa Amato, before commencing at the Bar in Sydney in 2008, was a solicitor for 7 years in Sydney and London. While in London, she was involved in some of the most significant defamation and privacy cases of the time and has established a practice in commercial litigation, defamation, intellectual property and media law.

Richard Scruby, who went to school from kindergarten to HSC with my son, and can be seen wearing my wig and gown around the traps, acquired a BA (Hons 1st Class and University Medal) LLB (Hons 1st class) at Sydney then won a scholarship to Oxford where he obtained a BCL (Hons) and M Phil. He is now at the Sydney Bar where he practises in a variety of jurisdictions, including equity and commercial law, corporations law, mining law and building and construction. Richard had this to say about his years of verifying: "I remember my time as a verifier as the point in my life when I actually started to get interested in practising the law. [Richard was then doing English Honours.] I don't quite know why, but learning technical rules about headnotes and case citation led to interest in the substance of the judgments and why one argument was thought by the Bench to be better than another".

Harriet Eager spent literally months working on the huge judgments in *Heydon v NRMA Ltd* [2001] 53 NSWLR 600 and had this to say to me on finishing work for the Council, "… I am a bit annoyed that I will never be able to look at a comma or full stop in the same way again — all that ticking, circling and underlining has changed my perspective for ever. I hope you get … to experience life beyond the green pen [a reference to the fact that I always used a green pen for editing]". Harriet is currently a partner at Minter Ellison and a specialist in Industrial Law.

What a joy and delight it was to have such skilled company for so long. We did learn a lot from each other. We exchanged books, recipes, ideas and lots more.

Producing law reports is very much about detail and pedantry. Heydon was uncanny in his ability to see the poor citation and the misplaced comma which had bypassed us all and save embarrassment down the track. I learned quickly from him. At times it has felt like a battle but as a number of judges, including Kirby P and Samuels JA, were kindly wont to acknowledge, "Even Homer nodded".

Judges, judgments and conversations

Contrary to popular belief, I have found all judges to be very human beings and have had some interesting correspondences and altercations with them over the years. I had and appreciated free and friendly entree and invitations to the Chambers of three Chief Justices, two Presidents of the Court of Appeal and any number of Justices of the Court. Frequently, after annual peripatetic meetings of the Consultative Council of Australian Law Reporting, I would report to the then Chief Justice. Chief Justice Gleeson was particularly supportive of the commitment of that Council to quality production and its endeavours to restrain proliferation of law reports. He would occasionally take the opportunity to seek guidance on matters raised with him by, for example, the publishers. Unfortunately I was not able to persuade him or his predecessor on the High Court of the need to address the gross disparity between the cost to the consumer of the authorised Reports of the High Court, the *Commonwealth Law Reports* (the CLR) and that of the NSWLR.

A couple of the consequences of the verification process were on occasions to seek from the judges a list of cases cited in argument but not contained in the decision and/or to seek verification in relation to perceived inaccuracies in quotations or other aspects of the written judgment. In 2004, Justice Greg James responded to one such request as follows:

> "Thank you for your letters recently seeking the list of cases cited in argument but not referred to in the judgment.
>
> We are lucky if we get a list of authorities, sometimes if we do, some of the cases in it are cited. Sometimes the citations in the list of authorities are accurate. Most of the time the references in argument are to: 'You know your Honour will remember it was that case which involved cats and the man with the gammy leg'.
>
> Particularly in such circumstances, it is difficult for me to let you have the case name and the citation. Often we don't get a transcript. Most of the time the cases cited aren't in the list of authorities and, as you have gathered, are inadequately referred to in the transcript. Often no transcript is provided or, if it is, the references to authorities appear in it as 'authorities cited' or 'authorities referred to'. This makes it very difficult for me to dig them out, especially months after I have sent the file back and someone sanitising it has thrown away the written submissions and such lists of authorities as might have been provided.
>
> I am sure in this context you will forgive me for not having any record or precise memory which would help".

In 1989, in connection with an enquiry, Justice Gordon Samuels said: "Some editor, whose name I forget said that he did not like living in a world full of misprints. Neither do I — neither do you. We must just keep battling along censoring everyone."

For a number of years Justice Dennis Mahoney and I carried on correspondence in relation to the writing of judgments and in 1996 he responded to some suggestions of mine in the following terms:

> "Thank you for your kind letter. It was cruel of you to remind me of what I once said, even though, if it was true: if you and I were in charge, things really would be different.
>
> I feel a little like Pope John XXII: so much to enjoy and so little time in which to enjoy it. But it will be fun to turn things upside down and see what happens.
>
> I have been thinking about the form of judgments. At a rough approximation the writing of a judgment takes 100 — 150%

of the time taken in the hearing of an appeal. I suspect there must be a better way of performing the functions which the preparation of judgments serves. What are your ideas? Can we start a new trend?"

and, in 1994, he responded to a query about a possibly incorrect citation:

"Most of the great things in life have come from imagination. I was once told that, in earlier times, men and women lay looking at the night sky and the millions of stars. With imagination, they were able to turn the complete confusion into systems and patterns and from this resulted Einstein, astronomy, and other wonderful things.

Similarly, in reading judgments the joy comes if one lies on one's back contemplates the inextricable confusion and seeks to find what really it is all about. In the present case, imagination shows that section 48(1)(d) meant section 48B(1)(c)."

In a printed judgment of Justice David Hunt, the Defamation Judge, in 1984, there appeared a statement in the headnote as to a "list of cases cited in the purported judgment". It should have read "reported judgment". In 1986, I received a letter in the following terms:

"This is a formal notice of a claim for damages for defamation. You have done it at last (although it was quite some time ago, I have only just noticed it)! You will have provided for my old age in comfort. My feelings are lacerated, and no doubt my reputation is in shreds. I refer of course, to the vicious and completely unwarranted attack upon the worth of my judgment in … in which you dismiss my worthy efforts (sob!) with the sneer that, despite the honesty with which I delivered it, it is no more than a 'purported' judgment.

I expect an offer of compensation forthwith, and (it is to be hoped) a correction (and apology?)."

My response to this headed "without prejudice" acknowledged his correspondence and stated: "Before retaining counsel in the matter may I submit for your consideration and approval a formal corrigendum which I undertake to have published as soon as possible. Yours in trepidation."

The response to this commenced: "Your letter of 14 November raises an interesting question. Although headed 'without prejudice', its contents were wounding in the extreme and its unjustified and unjustifiable composition is clearly relevant to my claim for aggravated damages … Nothing less than the most abject apology will suffice. You will notice that this letter is not written 'without prejudice'. Yours in despair …"

Detail and pedantry could have its light-hearted moments, thank goodness.

Other roles and activities — Education, training and advising

This is a list of some of the activities with which I became involved in NSW:

1982-1997 Editor *NSW Statutes Annotations* (Law Book Co Ltd) responsible for selecting and writing all annotation entries relating to the NSW Statutes from major series of law reports.

1982-1997 Editor ALMD (*Australian Legal Monthly Digest* — Law Book Co Ltd) responsible for digest entries for cases reported in NSWLR and various local government reports.

1988-1997 Editor of LGRA (*Local Government Reports of Australia*) subsequently LGERA *(Local Government and Environmental Reports of Australia*) responsible for selecting and reporting cases for all States of Australia other than New South Wales.

1991 Completed and published a *Manual of Law Reporting* widely used throughout Australia, New Zealand and the Pacific and used as a model for a similar Manual for the Republic of South Africa.

1991 By invitation, member and adviser to the Australian Institute of Judicial Administration Working Group on the production of a *Guide to Uniform Production of Judgments* published in 1992 by the AIJA and distributed to judicial officers throughout Australia; revised and republished in 1999.

1991 Provided advice to the Compensation Court of New South Wales on the establishment and publication of the *Workers Compensation Reports.*

1992-1993 Rewriting the title LOCAL GOVERNMENT for the *Australian Digest* (3rd ed) (Law Book Co Ltd).

1993 Provided advice to the judiciary and profession in the Republic of Vanuatu on the establishment and publication of a series of law reports for the Republic of Vanuatu.

1996 Invited to conduct a seminar on law reporting in New Zealand by the Council of Law Reporting for New Zealand.

Invited to conduct annual continuing education seminars on law reporting for the Bar Association of New South Wales. Provided advice in relation to establishing and/or publishing law reports in Vanuatu, ACT, and the Academy of Law in Singapore, and to the Industrial Commission of New South Wales.

1997 Invited by Judicial Commission of NSW to present paper on *Judgment Writing* to the Land and Environment Court 1997 Conference.

1997 Invited by the Consultative Council of Australian Law Reporting to draft a discussion paper on a *National Council of Law Reporting* for discussion by that Council.

1997 Appointed to the Legal Information Standards Council — a subcommittee of the Law Foundation of New South Wales.

1997-2000 Provided advice to the Industrial Commission of New South Wales on the updating of the Industrial Arbitration Reports.

1998 Appointed consultant on a pro-bono basis to the College of Law.

1999 Member of the advisory committee reviewing the *Council of Law Reporting Act* 1969 under the National Competition Principles Agreement.

1996-2006 Continuing Legal Education lectures for new barristers for Bar Association of NSW on topics of law reports and headnote writing.

2001 Invited by the Bar Association of NSW to contribute to the Bar Association's Centenary Essays project published as *No Mere Mouthpiece, Servants of All, Yet of None,* Edited by G Lindsay and C Webster, 2002.

Perhaps because I had become addicted to law reporting which, as I have said before, was in finding a less aggressive and hopefully more rewarding and family friendly way of using my knowledge and skills, I became involved in training reporters and providing information and advice to other bodies involved in law reporting, as listed above.

During this time I had responsibility for the quality and standard of headnote writing; for training reporters in headnote writing; for advising the Council on matters relating to law reporting; for liaising with the judiciary and the profession and the publishers in preparation and publication of the law reports. As honorary minute secretary to the Council I administered and co-ordinated the ever increasing activities of the Council including: negotiating publishing contracts and data licensing agreements; liaising with the Attorney-General's Department, other government departments and statutory bodies. For many years I co-ordinated the activities of the Consultative Council of Australian Law Reporting Bodies. This was a voluntary and unfunded Council, which brought together on an annual basis the Law Reporting Bodies of the various States and New Zealand, representatives of the Commonwealth Attorney-General, the Federal Courts and the Law Council of Australia. Its first meeting was held in 1983. It had three chairmen in my time, including Cedric Hampson QC, with whom I had read when first at the Bar in Brisbane. The major benefits from the annual peripatetic gathering were the mutual support for authorised and competently edited law reports, a continuing exchange of information and ideas and support for the practical education and training of law reporters and editors. The major and alarming deficit was probably the lack of interest from the professional groups and those they represented.

Entrepreneurship and Technology

In 1996 I instigated a policy strategy for the Council of Law Reporting under which the Council captured the then existing 75 volumes of the NSWLR onto a data-base to be authorised and licensed for digital use. I helped to guide that policy from conception through a completed tender process and co-ordination of the subsequent service agreements. By the mid-1990s the use of electronic versions of law reports was becoming well established and beginning to impact on the printed reports. There was much talk of converting the paper products to electronic versions which, of course, were much more searchable. I raised the matter with the Council's Solicitor, Margaret Calvert, who introduced me to Peter Meyer then of Desktop Law. Peter Meyer was able to lead us into and through the processes and systems which would need to be implemented to satisfy the Council objectives involved in recapturing the data from all volumes of the paper version of the NSWLR from 1969 and having that data marked up in such a way that it could be used with various forms of software and for various purposes. SGML (Standard Generalized Mark-up Language) was chosen as the generic form for this purpose. After spending a great deal of time perusing the reports in detail, Desktop Law was able to come up with an overall formula or formatting document from which the printing could be done. This document was called a DTD — a Document Type Definition — and was malleable when changes might become necessary.

The Council then advertised worldwide for expressions of interest in the conversion process. Specifications and tender documents were drawn up and circulated to a selected number of interested companies. Members of the Council, Project Manager Peter Meyer and I spent several days assessing and evaluating the tenders. Datamatics, a business in Mumbai (Bombay) India, was chosen and offered a contract for data capture and SGML mark-up for a fee fixed in Australian dollars.

Datamatics, represented by Suman Pai, completed the actual conversion in just over 12 months and produced an incredibly accurate electronic version of the reports. The process from creation of the original DTD through worldwide tender to delivery of the data took almost two years. A dedicated group of friends, reporters and research assistants checked for accuracy word for word, line by line and page by page in pairs for months. Data for the NSWLR thus became available to licensees/publishers for digital services. It was also marked-up in such a way that it would be feasible and relatively easy for licensees/publishers to cross-link portions of the NSWLR to products of their own. The Council then contracted with TurnKey Systems of Sydney for SGML mark-up and printing services for the continuing production using the same DTD. When the Council became self-publishing at Volume 51, I became a negotiator of licenses to use the data, commercial contracts with publishers, typesetters, printers, warehousers of paper and data and CD ROM producers. As the person supervising this electronic data conversion project I developed and implemented successful and enduring relationships with a large range and number of stakeholders and participants both within Australia and overseas. The success of the project led the Incorporated Council of Law Reporting for Queensland to undertake a similar process.

I consider that some of the most important challenges in which I have been involved were in this processes of turning paper products into electronic products. It was a very exciting area and era. I also enjoyed introducing other barristers and solicitors to the rigours of headnote writing and enjoyed my association with the Consultative Council of Australian Law Reporting from 1983 and the opportunities it provided to me to assist other Councils and other Editors especially by conducting meetings for Editors of law reports and reporters where I have been able to pass on some of my knowledge. I have enjoyed and continued to enjoy mentoring and keeping in touch with those young people who worked with me as research assistants in my various roles as Editor. It may have been a "lonely esoteric life" as Justice Heydon once described it but it was certainly much better than a "slog at the Bar for clients you never want to see again".

Appointed Editor of NSWLR

In April 2000, I was appointed Editor of the NSWLR on the elevation of Heydon QC to the NSW Court of Appeal. I retired as Editor and from the Bar in 2006 after just on 40 years as a practising barrister.

Regrets and disappointments

Not being a silk. I applied three times and was always knocked back, although I had assurances from three different presidents of the Bar Association that they would support my application and see it through. I knew that most of the Court of Appeal Judges were supportive, but because I wasn't appearing in robes and being seen in court it was not in the rules. The Editors of the English Law Reports are credited with silk because they are editors of Law Reports. I notice it doesn't appear to be on the Bar agenda in this country but is something that the profession here might like to take a look at.

Over the years of reading thousands of judgments and submissions put to the courts I noticed a continuing trend away from, advising on and pursuing how to comply with the law, to advising on how to avoid compliance. I see it continuing in the material I do see now and in media presentations. The only commendatory thought is that there are many young people who are enthusiastic to see that right is might.

Honours

In November 2005 there was a ceremonial sitting of the Supreme Court of Queensland to celebrate the centenary of the legislation which permitted women to practise as lawyers in that State. I received an invitation from the Chief Justice, Paul de Jersey, to attend and in his opening address the Chief Justice acknowledged my presence seated at the Bar Table with the Attorney-General as "the female barrister from this jurisdiction longest in practice".

After the proceedings two young women from the DPP at the Attorney-General's Department introduced themselves and in conversation asked if they could name a set of Chambers after me. It later transpired that they already had. The entry in the DPP Annual Report for 2004-2005 is as follows:

> **"Haxton Chambers**
> Haxton Chambers is named after Ms Naida Haxton, the first woman to practice at the Bar in Queensland. She received her first junior brief in the Supreme Court in 1967 and her first brief in the High Court in 1969. As well as maintaining a busy practice, Ms Haxton lectured at the University of Queensland. In 1971, following a move to Sydney, she practised at the New South Wales Bar and continued to lecture. From 1972 to 1981 she was also Editor of the Papua New Guinea Law Reports and in 1981 was appointed Assistant Editor of the New South Wales Law Reports. In 2000, Ms Haxton was appointed Editor of the New South Wales Law Reports."

In 2006, Leanne Clare SC, who was then Director of Public Prosecutions in Queensland, invited me to visit the Chambers and officially name them. It was interesting to see the way in which the Chambers worked and to talk with those who practised there. When I asked why they had considered naming Chambers after me, one young woman responded: "We think of you as a hero". I was very pleased to see that the majority of those in the Chambers were women. In 2010 I was invited to attend an occasion at the Brisbane Magistrates Court celebrating 25 years of the Office of the DPP in Queensland as an independent prosecuting office and recognised by the profession as one of the most significant improvements to the criminal justice system in the 20th century. The Annual Report for the year 2010-2011 notes that in the model of operation of each Chamber "is a self-contained legal team, in an integrated cycle of preparation, prosecution and support. The goals are continuity, consistency, efficiency and performance. The first Chambers established was Wakefield in September 2004, with Haxton, Sheehy, Sturgess, Given and Griffith established in 2005". Here I met up again with Des Sturgess, who was at the Queensland Bar when I was there.

In 2006, I was honoured as a Member of the Order of Australia for service to the legal profession and to the judiciary, particularly as the editor of the NSW Law Reports, and as a practitioner and educator.

In 2014, a Brisbane friend drew to my attention a different mention in a section of the *Courier Mail* titled *Headst@rt* and featuring Law Week in Queensland in which a Law Quiz had this entry;

> "6. Naida Haxton, Queensland's first practising woman barrister was admitted to the Bar in: a) 1928; b) 1966; c) 1989."

Some might think they have arrived when they are the subject of newspaper quizzes.

Relevant publications

Naida J Haxton: *A Manual on Law Reporting* 1991 published with assistance from The Federation Press and funding from the Law Foundation of New South Wales and republished in 2003.

N J Haxton: Law Reporting and Risk Management — Citing Unreported Judgments 2001, 185 ABR 84.

J M Bennett and N J Haxton: Law Reporting and Legal Authoring, *No Mere Mouthpiece, Servants of All — Yet of None*, LexisNexis Butterworths, Australia, 2002, 145.

Naida Haxton: Law Reporting: Rebutting some Assumptions: Law Book Co (2006) 80 ALJR 341

NJ Haxton: Editing judgments: lessons learned in the world of law reporting: Clarity (Journal of the international association promoting plain legal language) (2007) No 57 at 28.

Relevant references

Harriet Eager: Naida Haxton, *A Woman's Place - 100 Years of Queensland Women Lawyers*, Edited by Susan Purdon and Aladin Rahemtula, Supreme Court of Queensland Library, 2005.

Julie Lewis: Departing editor sounds alarm on state law reports: *Law Society Journal* (2006) Vol 44 No 5, 26.

Francis Douglas QC: Naida Jean Haxton — barrister and law reporter: *Bar News, The Journal of the NSW Bar Association — Winter 2006* at 67.

Helen Gregory: *Capturing law and history: One hundred years of Queensland Law Reporting*, Supreme Court of Queensland Library, 2007.

Civic Experience

1972-1982 Convenor for Laws and the Status of Women — National Council of Women for New South Wales.

1973-1974 Member of the Legal Subcommittee of the Women's Advisory Board (NSW).

1978-1979	Corresponding member of the Subcommittee on the Law and the Rights of the Child — IYC National committee of NGOs.
1986-1991	Representative of Shore School on NSW Parents' Council.
1998	Parish Councillor at St Thomas' Church, North Sydney.

If asked to advise young women today about a career in the law what would I say? The practice of law has changed so much since 1966. The skills may be still very much the same as they were back then but there is a lot more support, not personally, but in terms of the introduction of such things as Bar Practice Courses and compulsory continuing education. When I was lecturing to the Bar Practice Course in NSW the average age of new barristers was in the mid-30s. People were not coming, necessarily, straight out of university to the Bar. I think that some experience beforehand, even if it's non-legal, perhaps commercial or related, must be a major advantage. I think it's good to have some background that gives you a real sense of people and a real sense of what actually happens in the commercial world. And I think it's so much more important to know things like IT these days than ever before. Since the late 1990s I have mentored and helped my son in his business, an IT business, and I'm just so pleased I know so much about copyright and intellectual property contracts and things like that, but that just grew with the direction my career took. I didn't go out of university saying that's what I'm going to do. Someone contemplating a career in the law would need to be quite wise about what decisions they make because they could end up totally down the wrong path for them and unhappy with the outcome.

I would, however, recommend it as the most independent and challenging working life I could imagine and I have always cherished the freedom it provided me.

With Leanne Clare Director of Public Prosecutions at the opening of Haxton Chambers in 2006

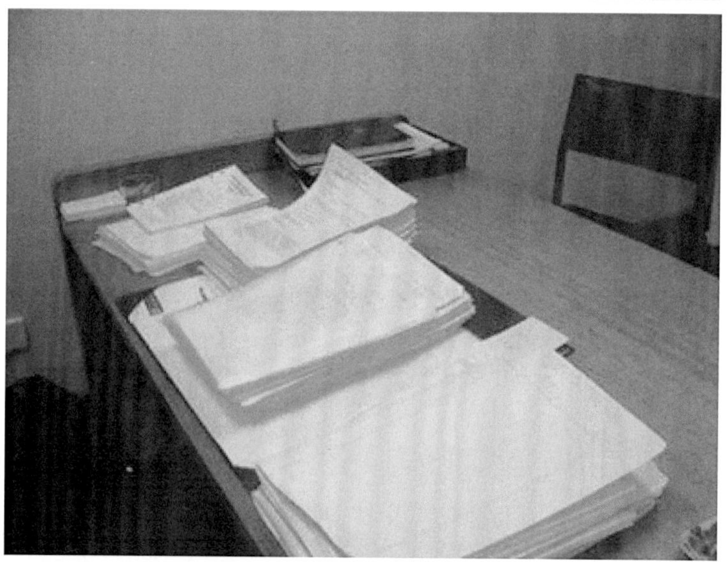

The Editor's desk on a typical day in 2006 - from left to right — published part to check on top of page proofs for approval, new judgments for reading, files ready for printer for approval and files with headnotes from reporters for approval.

On day of admission in Queensland, August 1966. Photo taken at home.

Chambers at Inns of Court in Brisbane 1966-1971 with rocking chair used by visiting barristers and mirror, so useful for checking one's hair.

Photo outside NSW Supreme Court on day of admission in NSW in 1972

Chambers at Frederick Jordan Chambers in Sydney in early 1974
wearing black pregnancy court dress.

Naida, 2005.

3. Things Ethical

Things Ethical — Philosophy — Ethics — Corporate work — Directorships — Committees — Chairmanship — Challenges — Involvement — Privilege and rewards — Rethinking religion

What is ethics? Ethics is basically about **doing** the right thing. One **does things** by habit or choice. Doing the right thing by habit may be a rare and idealistic notion. Doing the right thing by choice is another matter. It follows the making, either explicitly or implicitly, it is hoped, of a reasoned decision to do the right thing in situations that are often ambiguous, difficult and conflicted. When we as individuals have to make these decisions, we find small comfort in realising that these complexities are frequently a microcosm of situations that all society must deal with. Doing the right thing may or may not be effective or rewarding but is not to be avoided or replaced by unprincipled personal views or uneducated public opinion. In the modern world it is not so easy to do the right thing as often as one would like.

Growing up caring and sharing

I spent most of my early formative years in Cleveland. Cleveland was then a small country town beside the sea with a primary school — no high school — with families that went back in generations. It was a connected, mainly farming, community with a sense of purpose. I now see that sense of purpose in community and its families as — love thy neighbour — and do unto others as you would be done by. There was always enough to share, whether it was food, or cooking or help or advice; the local GP would call in on his way home to pick up a few vegies for dinner and ask if one of the children could go down to Mrs X tomorrow and see to her shopping as she was unwell; the police would stop to offer help when you had a flat tyre on the bike and put it in the back of the jeep and take you home; the same police were not far behind me when I rode past the station on my bike screaming my head off after having dived off the nearby jetty into the local swimming pool and into a Portuguese Man o' War; word went around when there were strawberries to pick and a shilling an hour to be earned. As we grew up we went to, and learned from, the local activities and opportunities: Sunday school; Church; Red Cross; Boy Scouts and Girl Guides; amateur dramatics; tennis clubs; doers of good deeds; you name it. All of these activities must have contributed to and must have reinforced the inherent motivation of the community in caring and sharing and doing unto others.

My cousin and I helped to do the flowers for church quite often because our home gardens had plenty of suitable flowers. My mother took a class in Sunday school. At some stage I became a Sunday school assistant and would practice what I was going to do in very simple classes at home. I recall with some embarrassment being banned from attending Sunday school for a week because I had used a swearword, which no doubt I had picked up from one of my brothers, but I had used it in the hearing of my mother. I still have a small Bible with minute printing that was presented to me as second prize for attendance at St Paul's Anglican Church Sunday School Cleveland and a book of common prayer, again with minute printing, presented as a "reward" in December 1951 when I would have been 10 years old. When I went to a Presbyterian Methodist high school at the age of 14, at each morning assembly the headmistress, Miss Taylor, provided a hymn, a reading and a short lesson. There were religious instruction classes and even a series on comparative religions. On Tuesdays there was something called self-denial for which we gave some of our pocket money to worthy causes. At college there was a morning prayer and a reading at breakfast, in which the senior students participated. Those students who were not at lectures might be asked to help with meals on wheels for the Presbyterian Church in Ann Street, Brisbane. There was always an opportunity and time "to do good". Church attendance became slightly more ecumenical. We tended to go to whichever church was appropriate for the time of day.

When it came to marriage, the Anglican Church in Brisbane refused to marry a divorced person but the Presbyterians were not so hidebound. In Sydney we attended a Presbyterian church in Manly for many years and with a move to North Sydney in 1991, joined the congregation at St Thomas' Church, North Sydney, where I was on the Parish Council in 1998. This year I was to discover that whatever decision the Parish Council made could be vetoed under the Synod Rules by the Minister. It did seem to be a rather undemocratic process. The teaching was very evangelical and there was little interest in involvement with the community beyond its own.

Introduction to Philosophy

It was 1993 when I attended a Cambridge University Summer School and chose moral philosophy and modern philosophy as two of my subjects for the duration and returned home intrigued by philosophy which I had never done at university and which I was keen to pursue. In 1995, I enrolled in a Graduate Diploma in Professional Ethics at the University of New South Wales. Here we discussed at length and in depth what ethics were and how they were to be applied in various areas of living and **doing,** what was involved in **doing** the right thing and how it applied to people, professions and corporations. I immersed myself reading books on philosophy, ethics and governance and wondering where I could use all this newfound knowledge. One of the topics we encountered related to in-house corporate thinkers or philosophers who would help employees in decision making, etc. This was an emerging idea in governance. I thought at the time what an interesting occupation that might be and have noticed with interest that it has morphed into philosophers in residence and seems to be very prevalent especially in schools in the USA. I made many attempts to find a position as a director and in the process found that it was not something that came easily. Recruiters were not very helpful unless, it seemed, they knew you or knew of you through their connections or you had experience as a director. Obtaining AICD (Australian Institute of Company Directors) qualifications seemed to be a compulsory prerequisite. I looked at the curriculum and found there was very little I had not done. The Graduate Diploma was unknown and virtually dismissed. Female directors were usually more than hesitant about sharing information or tips and one got the impression that they might have got positions from "mates" and had not needed to think too hard about how to get on to a board. Most people suggested starting with charities in order to get some experience. By 1998 I was in full project management mode for the digital conversion of the Law Reports previously noted and decided to put seeking a directorship on the side burner.

Early forays — Noggin

Son James goes on to complete Arts with Honours in Government, is selected for an Australian Advertising Award and spends a year in training with John Singleton in advertising. He then gets involved in student websites (Yap for those who may remember this incarnation). By 2000, James had become involved in an IT business, rather appropriately named Noggin, with a couple of friends from university days and I became a source of information on all sorts of matters including the drafting of documents and licences. For the first few years I kept the books of account. As the business was a great user of open source products, I managed to get my head around the legalities of using that kind of product, spending time in discussions with the Noggin owners. I have stayed in the background since then advising and helping wherever I can be useful.

BoysTown

In early 2004, completely out of left field came a late night phone call from Kathy Sullivan AM in Queensland. Kathy had joined the board of BoysTown on incorporation in 2003 and they were looking for a female lawyer who did not want to be paid for work-time lost on daylong meetings and, would I be interested? I knew BoysTown to be a long running major charity for marginalized youth and a service of the de La Salle Brothers in Australia but mainly through the BoysTown Art Unions. No remuneration other than "expenses" was on offer but they would include all costs of travelling from Sydney and being accommodated when necessary. Friends and family still living in Brisbane and opportunities to see them more often provided some incentive to consider the matter seriously. I did some research on the then current activities of BoysTown and the background to the de La Salle Brothers who owned and ran it and was invited to attend a meeting as an observer. I listened and decided that the work they were undertaking with disadvantaged youth was something which appealed to me and the business was somewhere I felt I could be useful. I was appointed as a director from the meeting on 15 July 2004. At that meeting, I asked the CEO: "Where is my induction kit?", to which the response was: "What is an induction kit?" Here was a challenge which became a two-way mutually rewarding process across 10 years.

In 2002 I had acquired what I considered a very practical book, *Boards that work: A new guide for directors,* by Kiel & Nicholson, 2002, McGraw Hill, Sydney. I bought an extra copy and gave it to the CEO. He bought copies for all the directors and ere long we were inviting Professor Kiel to speak to the board and Gavin Nicolson was running Governance and Strategic Planning Sessions. The book became the first item given to new directors. Addressing governance became somewhat of a priority.

In 2006 I became Chair of the Nominations Committee which subsequently broadened its role and became the Board Advisory Committee. I chaired this committee until retirement in 2013. I was voted Deputy Chair of the Board in 2009 and held that position until retirement.

My very first site visit was to Kids Helpline (KHL) counsellors where I spent the best part of an afternoon with a counsellor dealing with clients on the phone with a computer used to make notes for the record and with access continuously available on line to a supervisor. What an eye-opener that was. When it appeared that it might involve what is called a duty of care call, involving a decision to call in emergency services, the supervisor became personally involved. I was told how such calls were handled and how the local police would become involved. The number of duty of care calls increased considerably over the years I was there and was indicative of the need for the service and the remarkable service it continues to provide. Visiting client sites and taking part in activities brought home to me the impact and effectiveness that carefully structured programs can have on the lives of young people.

I visited the workplace site at Logan and learned about the fencing work in which clients, as the young people are called, were introduced to work experience either constructing or repairing wooden paling fences on State housing sites. We visited a site and saw the work in action. On one visit to Logan the board occupied a training room and, in our lunch break, I talked to a few of the clients about what they were doing. One young girl who was looking at job advertisements in a newspaper was actually more interested in "those people" getting out of the training room so "I can practise my interview". It is remarkable how effective listening to needs and applying a holistic approach can be and how receptive the young ones can be. My appreciation of the work of and dedication of BoysTown people was a very good reason to stay on.

As I lived in Sydney and there were offices at Blacktown and Campbelltown and a family refuge at North Richmond, I became a regular visitor to those sites and attended annual fundraising events at Bicentennial Park and the Hawkesbury Racecourse where once I even presented ribbons to the owners and trainers. One got to do lots of different and interesting things. In Queensland, I made a number of visits to Deception Bay where there was a very active parenting program, to Ipswich when undertaking job services programs started there, to Capalaba and other offices. In South Australia, I was house guest of the de La Salle Brothers in their facility at St Michael's College and introduced to the staff at the BoysTown offices in Adelaide and shown around their activities. I was then driven to Port Pirie where I was accommodated by Bishop Eugene Hurley in the church residence in what was described as the Pope's Apartment. Port Pirie was an early success story where, with the help of training from the local mining industry, young people were employed and the drop in juvenile crime in Port Pirie was acknowledged by awards from the police and the community. There was here also another very effective parenting centre. Later premises were provided for use in carpentry training including construction of such things as kitchen fit-outs and even extended into house building and repair. I returned to Adelaide and Port Pirie with the CEO for celebrations for the 50th anniversary of BoysTown in 2011. Getting to know the business and the people who managed and delivered it was essential and critical to the role of director as I saw it and I never hesitated to put in the time if I was available. In 2012, an Assembly of de La Salle Brothers from Australia, New Zealand and Papua New Guinea and representatives of lay partners was held over three days at Coogee. I was invited to take part. One of the main issues was the contemporary areas of youth need in Australia. After much discussion and relevant input on this topic a conclusion was reached that a major problem for youth could be attributed to a failure in parenting. BoysTown had had the foresight to see this as a need in establishing efficient and effective parenting programs whenever the opportunity arose.

Spending time with the management team provided opportunities to assess their skills and potential. Early in the piece I saw one long-term staff member as having unusual qualities and commitment but unfortunately no professional qualifications whatsoever. At a corporate gathering, over morning tea, I asked the question: "What does one do with someone who is CEO material but has no professional qualifications?. The answer I got was: "Send them to Harvard to do the management course". I passed this on to the CEO, enquiries were made and a proposal put to attend a course. The recipient was at the time a long-term employee with experience in many areas of the business and with a long-term corporate memory. She sat on my balcony in Sydney panic-stricken at not being able to do it, at never having sat in a formal lecture, never having sat an important exam and without financial qualifications. I gave her all the reassurance that I could that there would be plenty of individual attention and that with her practical experience she would not find it as difficult as she thought it would be. She was allocated a private tutor for financial matters and otherwise absorbed the experience to the hilt. She finished the course a transformed individual with the confidence to use the experience and the new found knowledge. I continued to give encouragement and support and delighted when she was selected as CEO on merit.

When I started, board meetings occupied the whole day and it was essential that time be devoted to introducing governance matters. It took close on two years to put in place a governance charter and committee charters. I took on the role of chair of the Nominations Committee and became the first in line to interview potential directors. Sitting on the other side of the desk was an interesting exercise. Some candidates offered their services quite directly thinking they could manage marketing or were on the lookout for a full management role. Women would often admit that they were looking for a directorship that would top up their income or superannuation. It was obvious that they had not looked closely at the company and its works. The Committee put in place a skills matrix which provided the requirements for skills needs on the Board and set about getting the desired balance. Some came on recommendations and others came via recruitment. Henceforth my legal drafting skills came to the fore with Corporate Governance and Committee Charters, related consequential changes to the Constitution and a Conflict of Interest and Related Party Transactions Policy. When the *Australian Charities and Not for Profit Commission Act* and Regulations came into effect the, by then, Board Advisory Committee addressed all documentation for compliance therewith.

By 2007 the Board was faced with finding a new CEO. A great deal of effort was put into working out what was needed for the right CEO for BoysTown by the Board and on my part a deal of reading on topics such as recruitment of CEOs and why CEOs fail. With a decision made to start with an internal recruitment, Br Ambrose Payne, as Chair of the Board, and me, as Chair of the Board Advisory Committee, spent 3 days interviewing the two candidates, assessing statements of claim to the job and talking to referees and stakeholders. What an interesting exercise to do and what a responsibility to undertake. The applicants then presented to the board. The effort put in certainly paid off with the appointment in early 2008 of Tracy Adams who proved to be exactly the right CEO for BoysTown.

Subsequent appointments to the Board, facilitated by engaging external recruiters, brought new skills and enthusiasms for the work. All new directors were employed readily on the committees and in providing 20 minute director development topics to board meetings. These topics included among others Strategy and Business Planning, ACNC Governance Standards, Marketing and the Boardroom, Executive Mentoring and Board Meetings and Minutes, which complemented topics from management on, eg, Leadership Development and Measuring Social Impact. We were not only using our skills as directors but educating each other in the process. After I was appointed Deputy Chair of the Board there were a number of times when I was called upon to chair the board in the absence of Br Ambrose and one occasion on which I chaired an Independent Directors Meeting. As a group we got to enjoy each other's company and to appreciate the skills contributed. Strategic planning time was spent annually, usually at one of the BoysTown sites, and proved to be informative, stimulating and productive. At one of my last strategy days we promoted the introduction of Efficiency and Effectiveness Reports across the delivery of services for the board. The staff took up the challenge and, by the time I left, the board was beginning to see and appreciate exactly where every cent was spent and how effectively all that fundraising was being used. The emphasis placed by the CEO and management on evidence-based material as the foundation for programs, reports and submissions has my enduring admiration. The Annual Kids Helpline (KHL) Insights into Australian Young People which produces evidence of the top issues affecting children and young people who contacted Kids Helpline in the previous year is made available for use by other services dealing with young people around Australia. I was delighted to be asked to attend the launch of the 2014 report in 2015 at the Opera House in Sydney.

Over Christmas 2009-2010 Br Bill Firman, who had been on the Board, had gone to Southern Sudan to help in establishing a Catholic Health Training Institute at Wau in Southern Sudan in relation to the Solidarity with Southern Sudan (SSS) Project. He sought my help to assist in drafting a workable Constitution for the Institute. The Institute's aim is to train Sudanese health professionals who would provide an adequate and improving health care service for the people of Sudan, inspired by the Christian vision of the dignity of the human person and based on the values of respect, compassion, justice and solidarity. Lengthy emails passed to and fro over many weeks the result of which was to provide me with the means of understanding the aims of the SSS project and the rules of the Church in relation to the establishment of such a body. It was indeed a challenge both as to content and drafting. I was more than delighted the following year to hear that it had all been adopted by the Church in Rome without any issues being raised. A teacher training institute was subsequently added. I still look forward to Br Bill's regular reports on progress which include details of graduations, life as it must be lived in such a disturbed country and photographs of young people who do not seem to be dispirited by the happenings around them.

In 2012-2013, I set about finding a replacement for myself — a female lawyer who would be happy to give time without remuneration. The happy person was Kristan Conlon who is a partner of a leading independent Australian law firm with a background in property and corporate advisory. The minutes of the last meeting I attended contained the following vote of thanks:

> "We record the enormous example of public spirit that Naida has modelled for us. It is a spirit that has been totally unselfish with not a skerrick of self-serving, marked by an integrity that has won everyone by reason of its total ingenuousness and absolute sincerity."

I was farewelled at the Annual Board Dinner in November 2013. Along with a gift voucher for an Art of Nature Experience in Tasmania, I received a card filled with embarrassingly kind and appreciative handwritten notes reflected in the following email after the meeting from Peter Ffrench:

> "A few lines on a card and a quick farewell after dinner hardly seem sufficient to express my thanks for your support at

> BoysTown over the past three years. I rarely attempt to predict the future, but can be confident in forecasting there will be many times next year and beyond when someone around the Board table expresses words to the effect of "we need Naida for this! … or what would Naida say?" We will miss your strength and compassion, your insight and experience, your wisdom and above all, your unquestionable integrity. … Thanks for your support, quiet yet assured guidance, and counsel."

When I was invited to join the Board of BoysTown in 2004 I had no idea that I was joining a community motivated by the same sense of commitment to community, to caring and sharing, which I had savoured growing up in Cleveland and had tried to follow all my life. As I left, I was overwhelmed by the pursuit of caring and sharing epitomised by the works of BoysTown and the de La Salle Brothers in following the founder, John Baptist de Salle, in acting "sensitively and courageously on behalf of young people". A fellow director said of the mission at a strategic planning session: "It was about good people doing good works for good outcomes". It was a very real privilege to have been part of being and doing BoysTown for so long.

Strata living

I bought into a home unit building in 1999. When I retired from practice in 2006 I was invited to join the Executive Committee (EC) of the Owners Corporation mainly because I was a lawyer and might know how things should be done. In 2008/9, I became Chair and Secretary. I bought a book on Strata Management and Law. I went to an Executive Committee training session. I took the role seriously, got to know the building and its needs, negotiated over fire orders, dealt with contractors and lawyers and allowed it to take up too much of my time and energy. In 2014 I resigned after having been told at an EC meeting that everyone in the building hated me and then called by every swear word invented as well as threatened. Who would want these positions? Behaving properly and ethically did not seem to be on the agenda. When I tried to get those on the EC (all from professional backgrounds) to declare their conflicts of interest (of which there were many) at each meeting, I was told in no uncertain terms that the Owners Corporation was not anything like a company and those principles did not apply because the EC was "just a committee". When one is outvoted one is outvoted regardless of law or ethics. New legislation, now passed, tries to ensure that standard corporate responsibilities apply. Let's hope it is effective to do so.

Rethinking religion

Early in the new century and with a huge amount of philosophical reading undertaken, I began to question what religion really meant to me. I think that a catalyst was a sermon on the conversion of Saul the Apostle, on the road to Damascus, from which I came away feeling that the message had been that, without some revelatory conversion, one was not worthy to be a Christian. I started to delve into the history of Paul and the history of the Bible as Gospel. I slowly concluded that Paul conducted perhaps the greatest advertising campaign of all time to secure the acceptance of the Old Testament as Gospel. What it was more probably was no more than a collection of orally handed down and recorded memories open to being reinterpreted from time to time to reflect feelings more than reason. I moved on to other books on religion and God and Christianity notably authored by Grayling, Onfrey, Dawkins, Spong, Tony Windrow and, the book that upset me most, by Geraldine Brooks, *Nine Parts of Desire*, dealing with Islam and women. That the suppression of thought, education and commerce should be glorified and attributed to Allah made no sense whatsoever. Paul Collins, in *Believers — Does Australian Catholicism have a Future?*, discussed the growing scepticism of church as an institution. Tony Windrow, in the *Thoughtful Guide to Faith*, elucidated the thinking about God, the Bible, Church, Prayer, Creed, Holy Communion, baptism, marriage, funerals, Christmas, Easter, miracles, death, soul and doubt, along the way drawing distinctions between Christianity and Churchianity. I concluded at the end of the day that one could **be** a Christian, live a moral or ethical life and **do** good without having the trappings of a being a church goer and gave up going to church. It was *A Guide to the Good Life - The Ancient Art of Stoic Joy*, by William B Irvine, that set me on a path of considering a philosophical life rather than what I had been wont to think of as a Christian life or a religious life. I decided that I had probably been a practising stoic most of my life and left it at there.

The question of ethics in conduct has become one of the most challenging issues confronting the community today. We see professionals, business people, the public services, academia, trades and society generally addressing the challenge. We see and hear increasing discussion about issues involving ethics. We study philosophies, policies and procedures in the hope of affirming, developing, improving, renewing and refining those philosophies, policies and procedures. We look for external assurances as standards and encourage the production of codes of ethics, codes of practice, rules and regulations and, if all else fails, statutory controls. All of these issues, events and principles involve individuals whose daily interactions and decisions together make an impact on the ethics of our social structures. I have concerns for these individuals because of the complexities of modern living which seem to be attracting a diminishing regard for personal integrity and personal responsibility for making value decisions. Much of this would seem to be engendered by the growing accessibility to external value controls and decision making processes. This then impacts on the availability of resources to the system as a whole. In a sense it abrogates ethics from individuals. Codes and practices, rules and regulations are fine for communicating expectations; they do not provide guidance on how specific decisions involving ethics can be made: they do not even provide guidance on how to start thinking ethically. And we fund Commissions of Inquiry into misbehaviour with great regularity.

And governments, sadly and misguidedly, do not see the need to encourage the development of ethics in schools. Perhaps if it was called philosophy the arguments against might disappear.

BoysTown clients at work on refurbishing State housing in Adelaide

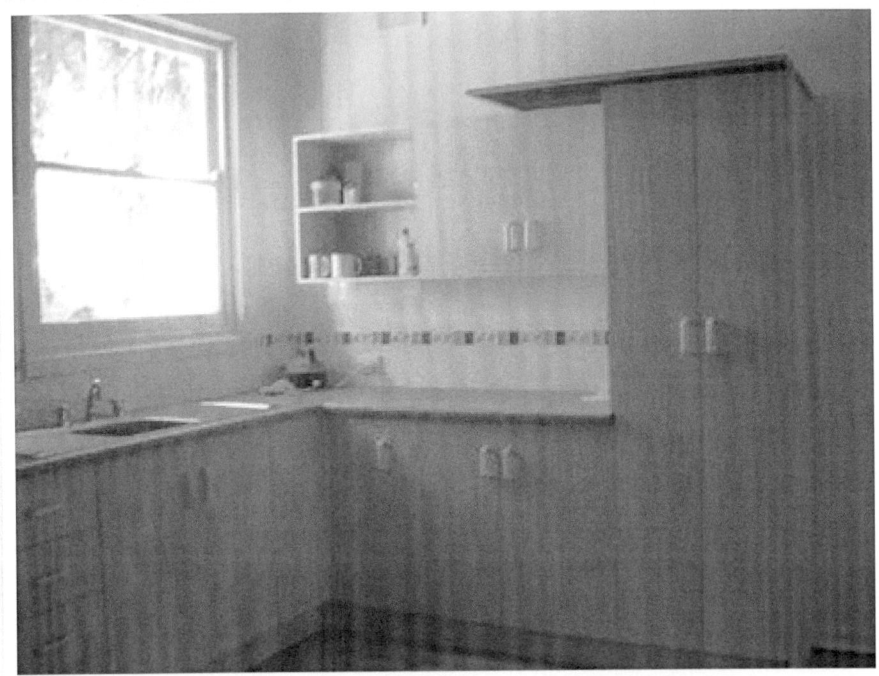

Kitchen built by BoysTown clients in Port Pirie and installed in refurbished State Housing in Adelaide

With David Field, BoysTown Ambassador, at Sydney function 2011.

With Miranda Kerr, Kids Help Line Ambassador at launch of KHL program in 2011 in Sydney.

4. Things Romantic

Things Romantic — Courtship — An affair of the mind — Marriage — Family — Theory and Reality — Things less romantic

In my 1895 *Lloyd's Encyclopaedic Dictionary* the word "romantic" is stated to be something to be attributed to extravagant or fanciful ideas without any reference whatsoever to something like "love". With the passage of time, in 2015, the *Macquarie Dictionary* has introduced the concept of "romantic affair or experience; a love affair". As Michael Kirby, when President of the Court of Appeal in New South Wales, once assured me, English is an evolving language and his use of a particular word in a judgment which I had questioned had changed and evolved with the passage of time. In this sense, things romantic in my life have gone through a process of evolving with the passage of time.

Early introduction

My early introduction to things romantic can strangely be linked to medical issues. When I was nine I broke my leg and spent three months at home with my whole leg in full plaster to stabilise the knee and, on crutches, before I could return to school. During that time I read the local library out of all appropriate or suitable books for a nine year old, much to my mother's frustration at the time. Some four years later I severely strained that same leg and was once again on crutches for at least three weeks. This time, my mother attended the library to find books that would be more suitable for me to read. She managed to find some very mild-mannered adult "romances". What a world of wonder was revealed to me!!

In my first year at university I had an appendectomy instead of doing a Pure Maths 1 examination. Consequently there was a deferred examination often called a "post" during the vacation. I took myself off to study at the university library and to the end of the book stacks underneath a window where there was good light, a comfortable desk and little likelihood of disturbance. In a moment of boredom I looked up to my right, and discovered a whole range of books on courtship and marriage. Consequently the study of mathematics became neglected in proportion to the degree of interest that the diversionary tactics of reading these books involved. Here was very practical advice on how courtship should be conducted, on how one should become conversant with the extended family of any romantic interest in order to avoid any disappointments in the future, on how important having the same moral and ethical background was, on philosophical discussions of romance and infatuations, the historical and religious background, etc, etc.

One of those books was that of Bertrand Russell entitled *Marriage and Morals* where, in an edition I later acquired, (1972) ed, George Allen and Unwin) he had this to say (at 37):

> "The essential of romantic love is that it regards the beloved object as very difficult to possess and as very precious. It makes therefore greater efforts of many kinds to win a lover of the beloved object, by poetry, by song, by feats of arms, or by whatever other method may be thought most pleasing to the lady. The belief in the immense value of the lady is the psychological effect of the difficulty of obtaining her, and I think it may be laid down that when a man has no difficulty in obtaining a woman, his feeling towards her does not take the form of romantic love. Romantic love is, as it appears in the Middle Ages, was not directed, at first, towards women with whom the lover could have either legitimate or illegitimate sexual relations; it was directed towards women of the highest

respectability, who were separated from their romantic lovers by insuperable barriers of morality and convention. …

The Renaissance had, however, learnt from the platonic love of the Middle Ages to employ poetry as a means of courtship."

(and at 41)

"I believe myself that romantic love is a source of the most intense delights that life has to offer. In the relation of a man and woman who love each other with passion and imagination and tenderness, there is something of inestimable value, to be ignorant of which is a great misfortune to any human being."

In about 1964, whilst an articled clerk, I discovered that the bookkeeper in the law firm where I was an articled clerk possessed all of the books of Georgette Heyer which she kindly lent me two at a time until I had devoured the lot. The intrigue in these traditional "romances" lay in the essential romantic plot, where the female protagonist nearly always wanted to marry for love, with little reference to or discussion of sex, but plenty of room to let loose the fanciful imagination on an endless number of possibilities. There was always plenty of tear-jerking material.

So when "romance" entered my life, what happened, what did I **do**?

An Affair of the Mind

In his eulogy to David Boddam-Whetham, in 1994, Hartley Anderson, a nephew, said this:

"He moved to Brisbane in the late sixties, taking the boys with him. It was here he met the young barrister, Naida Haxton, with whom he had *an affair of the mind* for nearly two years before they married in 1971. … There was Bin the husband — Naida says the relationship is best described in terms of the wedding ring he designed. Three bands of gold joined together signifying — YOU, ME, and US in the middle. They gave each other space but were united and productive together."

When I was collating an inventory of David's papers after his funeral, I found all the letters I had written to him in a folder. I had kept all the letters I had received from him in a folder. I took them all with me on a short holiday, settled down to sort them chronologically and cried on and off for four days. "Romance" had not deserted me.

And so to a few extracts from that *affair of the mind*, poetry and homespun philosophy included, from me in Brisbane and often from David all over the country and the world (me in italics, David in normal font).

This morning I found your rose had died
No mourning,
For it shall be decried
A red rose
It was and shall always be.
You chose
It, alone for simplicity,
Rosebud red,
For purity and loveliness,
In a bed
Of heather, for solitude,
Deep, deep red,
Bashful shame that means;
Left unsaid,
Was so much it seems.
Little knowing
Its giving had meaning so deep,
Little showing
A moment to treasure, to keep.
No mourning
For something meant to live long.
This morning
Its passing burst into song!

... A rose may be a catalyst —- whatever that may be. One need not look for reasons why a catalyst should work, except appreciate that it is necessary and has value. For "value" I have no definition. Value in the context I have used it is absolute, unrelated to ordinary values — and all I know is that it exists, much like the song from a rose.

People who have written to me over the years know I have an uncontrollable urge to reply to letters when and as I receive them. ... Poets who talked of "emotions recollected in tranquillity" spoke myriads of both the small and the large things of life, and perchance, if we were able to look carefully enough we would find a definition for your all elusive "value". There are today three things I value dearly:-

My family, — my mother was very close to me last night and it is partly for her that I write this letter for she gave me standards with value.

Myself: selfish perhaps but not trite; nor trite to talk of loving work that has helped to make me into the person I am, but also a part of me; a part that cannot be allowed to wither or die. It is a completeness which could, in this suburban community, be easily spoiled!

Knowing you: which chronologically and value-wise is third on the list ...

[When an American landed on the moon on 20.7.69 a long essay like letter arrived beginning thus:]

Man on the Moon! How synonymous to that strange man we used to point out to our children —- the Man in the Moon. Indeed it is a popular, but ancient legend that the Man was put there for gathering sticks on a Sunday, yet through the ages people have worshipped, gazed at, written about, dreamed about, speculated about and written songs about the Moon. Bing Crosby sang, "I wished on the Moon for something I never knew, I wished on the Moon for a dream to come true ...". He was in a bad way, but the Moon was his catalyst. The moon cursed by man when he wanted darkness — the moon the saviour of many men who needed light in the darkness. Stories of it are infinite. ... It is the inner self rejection of what we possess — this eternal seeking — this continual scanning of the man on the moon — this continual reaching for the moon that breathes into us the spirit that makes life really worthwhile. [to which the response was:]

To a man on the moon,
I may be silent, but
I'm thinking.
I may not talk, but
Don't mistake me for a wall.
I may not communicate, but
I'm still here
And the moon may be very far, but
It's very near
From a woman on earth.

[There was often talk of being alone which, on occasion, prompted more verse:]

There are occasions on which I may be alone
Not in the company of others
By myself
In solitude

Single
Isolated
Individual
Solitary
Unaccompanied
Unattended
Azygous.
There are occasions on which I will be thought to be so.
There are occasions on which I will appear to be so.
There are occasions on which I will be so.

[There were prolonged discussions on empathy:]

Empathy — To see with the eyes of another,
To hear with ears of another
And to feel with the heart of another.
What do we ordinarily derive from empathy?

It helps us to understand other persons from within. We communicate on a deeper level and apprehend the other person more completely. With this kind of communication we often find ourselves accepting that person and entering into a relationship of appreciation and empathy (!). In another sense empathy becomes for us a source of personal reassurance. We are reassured when we feel that someone has succeeded in feeling himself into our state of mind. We enjoy the satisfaction of being understood and accepted as persons. It is important for us to know, to sense that the other person not only understands our words but appreciates the person behind the message as well. We then know we are recognised and accepted for the particular kind of person we are. When friends fail to empathise we feel ourselves disappointed and rejected. We want people to listen to us empathically, even if they are familiar with what we are going to say. We look for a feeling response and, when that is lacking, we feel that something is wrong with the personal relationship. The exchange of verbal messages is not always enough for us.

We look for a correspondence of mood. When we find it in face to face meeting with friends, when we sense it in reading the words of Shakespeare or in a favourite psalm, we are less lonely and more content. When empathy is lacking our self-awareness and self-respect are diminished. We then experience ourselves more as objects and less as persons!

[There were frequent discussions on "home", "family" and "parents":]

Home is home. It is security in relation to material comforts, people and being alone.

It is different to other places in that it is more attractive. It is perhaps less ordered, but not disorderly. It is a place of ordered existence and ordered living — the "order" comes from love, harmony, presence and example — that is what gives standards and values that can be adopted, applied, ignored or fought. Where these standards are missing or not fully achieved it is only right to accept the fact that children must flounder.

If a family is to be successful (perhaps the word is happy — but at any rate it should not be floundering) the family maker should be there with love, harmony, presence and example when needed, which could be anytime. If it has to be made it might as well be made properly, with the best materials and workmanship available and the making might as well be enjoyed. Give to yourself at home, some of the things you enjoy, and need, and want. Enjoy them there, and perhaps others will share and seek to share your pleasure in being there. Home should be a place where the time to share is unimpaired.

Let me tell you a little about my home —

Home is a place one can always go back to, and the knowledge that no matter what you have done, or what has happened, you will be given whatever can be given.

Home is a place which has routines, sometimes annoying ones, but routines which are frequently missed when they are not there. It is these routines which one endeavours to perpetuate as standards when one is on one's own.

Home is a place where one can be one's self, yet in being so, preserve dignity and respect for others within the family.

Home is a place where one may have differences, and share differences — but at all times be loyal to the family when the outside world intervenes.

Home is a place of many choices — one can start something and never finish it — one can work on something to almost the exclusion of everything else — one can do some dreaming and not necessarily attain — one can speak one's ridiculous thoughts and not be humiliated — one can be illogical yet understood — one can be untidy but not to the detriment of others.

Home is a place that other people like to come to — a place where the youngies like to talk to the oldies.

Home is a place that is built individually and in combination with.

Home is to be shared.

Home is a place that has food in the refrigerator at all times — a meal in the oven no matter when one returns home — a tin of biscuits that never empties.

Home is a place where one can put footprints on the ceiling and no one minds.

Home is where you can fall asleep in front of TV.

Home is a place where people can laze around in their pyjamas on Sunday morning, read the papers and have tea and toast in the sun.

Home is a place where it is sometimes better to draw the water from the well rather than have a modern chrome plated water tap in every room.

Home is a place where on certain days there is the same old thing to eat — one complains when it is available and one complains when it isn't.

Home is a place to potter — a place to be with — a place for mutual relaxation and accomplishment — a place for mutual being together.

Perhaps I can tell you more some other time.

A parent is someone who is THERE. Whether or not they are needed or wanted is immaterial. ... You CAN translate the best of yourself and the best of what you can give though by being A PARENT and providing the continuity, the security, the needs, and the "presence" of a home; you do not have to do it all yourself; provided you provide, you fulfil your appointed tasks. You may think that the material provision of everyday living is unrewarding and time consuming, and time wasting and ... but it has to be done, it is man's work — it can be done and the more rewarding things you seek follow naturally — it's something like the same plants, the same soil, the same weather but one nurtured and the other not. One MUST NEVER lose sight of the fact that children are GROWING UP, not grown up — and they need nurturing. Some very good plants grow in hot-house conditions; and many decent adults have grown up in artificial surrounds or socially deficient surrounds.

I can only say that I believe that "being a parent" is a job, a task, work; it can be a chore, at times a nuisance, a bore; but it is also a charge, a caring and a duty; it is first a doing and only secondly a being.

[The immediate family often referred to David as the "Fother" as he tried so hard to absorb the missing role of a mother with that of the present father. Subsequent letters covered resettling in Sydney; finding a home; schooling for the boys, the "mechanics of it all"; family in Sydney; books; radio and TV programs; the "doings" of many days interspersed with previously discussed matters and new topics. In January 1969, David returned to Sydney with his three sons who had been in boarding school in Queensland and there began a year of fleeting visits and over 180 long, short and frequent letters to and from. The first letter was from No 1 son thanking me for "for the tremendous box of food you gave us before we left for Sydney. There was enough for both lunch and dinner and it was really delicious". And the correspondence continued:]

Last night was to the President's reception at … and Dame Annabelle Rankin delivered a very thoughtful and well prepared paper on "Education for Living". The message which I got was that "we" must be educated to think, and it is in reaching a stage where the thinking is meaningful that is the ultimate achievement. Meaning must be full of those values we are always talking about but, provided it is meaningful, it must be worthwhile and does it really matter whether it is highly objective or not. When we cease finding "value" anywhere — then we ought to think about how we are limiting God.

…

Just watched the religious program "Directions" on TV. It was titled "To be is an active verb" it was produced by the Jewish theological seminary of America. It was good — so good that my mind is turning over and over; exceptionally well produced — and up to the minute with the conflict between the parents "you should" and the child's "why". Although the problem is far, far deeper than a sense of spiritual wellbeing, it proposed the huge question — how can children find their way if their parents can't — and the addition of course is, if their parents can't give them some sense of direction. The part answer to that question was: parents must always be learners as well teachers. The ultimate conclusion from a personalised purely subjective question was — Hernani — I am here — to be is an active word. I am here not just to do, but to be; there is hope only if I risk myself for it; to be is the joy of sensing one's self in the presence of the divine! Good!!

Perhaps I should heed your "value" warning — viz, "when we cease finding value anywhere — then we ought to think how we are limiting God". Then, perhaps anywhere is the operative word. I can find value almost anywhere — even in this job of mine — I'm helping to make all the Managers and Town Clerks "better people" and thus contributing something. But they can be so bloody pig headed, unco-operative and astutely perverse (must get this spelling right) and even perverted — but sometimes I would like to bonk them on the head with the biggest leaden mallet available. However, not to worry, because if I write a book about them, they will be my subjects and I not theirs. …

What can I do with your letters? I file them in the front of my main file. Everything that is incomplete, pending action, or "don't know quite what to do with", goes in the front of my main file. Then occasionally when I'm in the mood, I will transfer them to another file (perhaps). I really don't know what to do. If you wish I shall seal them up and put them with my diaries …

[Then David and the boys moved into their new home at Fairlight and the homespun philosophy continued.]

Just to say: Happy Days in the new house with lots of new rooms and views and nooks and crannies and everything to be tried out at once and doors to be opened and shut and boxes and cupboards to be emptied and filled and lots of shouting and excitement:

Where will I put this chair?
Will someone come up here?
I've caught my trousers on the stair
It will fit never fear
I'm hungry Dad, what's to eat?
Did anyone think of meat? …
It will never fit, it will never fit!
Very well, but just don't sit
If necessary we will move the wall
I can hear it all
And outside the wall, and on the fence
A box for letters — any perchance?
I hope it arrives in time to welcome you all to the Fairlight mansion
Happy days. …

On parenting … It seems to me that what is lacking in this world is the ability of parents and adults to say "no", with effectiveness, because they themselves have deprived the word of any significance or meaning. With it has gone the foundation of standards and values; they have not lost respect but have never earned any; kids today may be "better educated" in the sense that they are fed more information than were their parents for the simple reason that there is more information available — but they are not taught how to use it properly; or should I say they have no standards except a self-orientated one by which to use it. "Self-expression" can't even develop self-awareness in this sense. The great awakening is reflected in the endless childish questioning of "why can't I", to which no answer is really expected; to which no answer is satisfactory because when it could have had any impact and laid any foundations at the age of two or so, there was no answer, because there was no question, because they were then "self-expressing" themselves without any guidance. Why should they need it now? ...

Me: "Please send some flowers to Miss H for me."

Girl at the florists: "We've done this for you before - hasn't she said 'yes' yet?."

Me: "It is purely a token of appreciation for some work she has done for us."

Girl: "How dull — I was getting all romantic."

[Somewhere around early December 1970 we agreed to get married ... I recall agreeing to do so provided I did not change my name or compromise my standards!]

Thank you for the gorgeous, gorgeous, gorgeous roses that were sitting on my desk when I came back from court at lunchtime. Their presence in my room has created quite a stir to the extent that I was asked in the Common Room at lunch time "if there was any truth in the rumours that my chambers would shortly be up for sale because I would be going to further climes!!!" I do not quite know what to make of that one.. .

[On 22 January 1971 we were married in Brisbane and left by car a couple of days later for Sydney, and to the home at Fairlight. The boys followed with friends some days later and the first activity was organising their return to boarding school. This did not mean the end of the correspondence. Within the first month:]

Marriages are conventionally times for happiness and the sharing of the happiness, the excitement and the pleasures of giving and receiving. It brings in its wake a one way flow of thankyou letters. To the ones I have already written I add this one to you and for you.

Our marriage may not have had all the external paraphernalia of the conventional; and you expressed a firm desire that we should not give to each other anything which would materially signify the event, that there should be no gifts, no presents, no tokens, given or taken, beyond the giving and receiving of ourselves and each other. For your firmness I am very grateful.

At a time indeed when people were enthralled with the use of words and perhaps their novelty and effectiveness, Crabb discriminated between "gifts" and "presents", describing a gift as an act of generosity contributing to the benefit of the receiver and describing the present as an act of kindness courtesy or respect, contributing to the pleasure of the receiver.

In this light wedding "gifts" may be regarded as gifts contributing to the material benefit and comfort of the couple, and also as presents contributing much to the pleasure and status of the couple. With it all, the opening of parcels, the untying, the unwrapping and seeing the contents gives to all of us a special within-ourselves-pleasure. If opened in the presence of the donor it gives a special between-ourselves-pleasure. Each parcel brings, and each additional parcel adds to, an aura of pleasurable excitement, delightful anticipation and a glowy aftermath, and an urge to go on reopening the parcel until the contents are truly familiar.

[In retrospect, I have concluded that while courtship may be a romantic pursuit, marriage is a job, unfortunately without a job specification, requiring hard work, attention to detail and some definite boundary setting. There continued very sporadic correspondence for many years, some of it romantically inclined but much of it devoted to "family" issues and the differing perceptions of the practicalities of organising day to day living particularly with regard to the duality of needs of teenage boys with a mother not far away.]

When people marry they should not forget or overlook, by virtue of other demands — that they were once single, and that by dint of circumstance they came together, came to love one another and then decided to make their lives together.

I write this to myself — not that it is necessary, except that I would like you to know that I have had this thought. So with three days of weekend almost on us, let us have a little time together to reinforce the concepts which brought us together.

[Throughout his life David kept up a practice of finding time each evening to sit at his desk, write up his diary and record his expenses for the day. He would then write a note to someone remembering a birthday or anniversary, passing on a thought or "something that you might be interested in" or just replying to a letter received in the mail. Or sometimes a note to me:]

And now the end of another era in your life.

You came from Brisbane — you put the house right — you've started a practice and built it up to a success. In all these things you can be proud within yourself, for indeed I am proud of you.

You now start out on another adventure — to be a mother — I am pleased for your sake (and my own) and even more so for the baby, because

I think you will make a good Mother. And finally, I will miss having you in town for occasional meetings and on the spot advice.

In all things I am really a very lucky person — not only do I realise it but other people tell me so.

[And sometimes a note from me:]

I awoke this morning feeling like a mother: it was a warm glowing and very complete feeling. I think our son is perfectly gorgeous.

You have made me somebody's mother!! It seems somehow that for the time being anyway you have put me slightly away from myself and yourself. There are always others around or things to do and so it will be no doubt for the next week, and I am accepting it, though I do long to be home …

Get on with your things for a while and don't spend all of your time trying to do it my way: it is of so little significance.

Life after motherhood

And so began another adventure in living and doing, of melding into yet another family unit. It did give rise to some anachronistic experiences such as the Higher School Certificate before kindergarten. Somewhere along the way we seemed to reach consensus on most issues despite David and I having totally different ways of approaching many of them. My approach to many things, especially where I was in unfamiliar territory, was (inherited from my mother) to say "no" if in doubt — a no can safely be turned into a yes but the reverse does not work well. David's approach was far more spontaneous and far less structured. The older boys cajoled and begged until allowed to leave boarding school to become day boys: No 1 came home for his last term of high school; No 2 chose to live with his mother to finish high school; No 3 finished high school and then chose to live with his mother "to find out what it was like". Whilst in residence they all became reasonably willing workers and contributed to cooking, washing-up, ironing, house renovations and other activities, even if not always as enthusiastically as father would like.

Much of our weekends revolved around 22 years of schoolboy sport. I think I might have travelled to pretty well every cricket pitch and football field in Sydney by the time James finished high school. At the age of 52, David agreed to captain the Manly Cricket Club fifths and a few more ovals were added to the list. Many weekends were filled with exeating country boarders: this continued until James left Shore in 1991. We had decided to send James as a weekly boarder at the age of nine, so that I could maintain a full practice at the Bar. This worked well for me but not necessarily for James. Whether or not it was a good decision, one will never know but it did not seem to impact negatively on his progress. By the end of first year in high school he was ready and able to come home as a day boy.

When the boys turned 18 each insisted on having a party at our home, each choosing a menu which I was required to produce: No 1 a formal dinner for 15: No 2 an oriental themed evening for about 50 odd; No 3 a lunch for 50 odd with meat loaves and favourite sweets' dishes. When it came to James' turn he would not hear of me engaging a caterer. James had tagged along and probably became what David would have called "street wise" in some areas of life long before it was at all wise for him to have done so. He was into cooking curries and curries were what the guests had. As many as could came "home" to celebrate Christmas until about 2004, when the older boys/men had acquired families of their own and were themselves heading into grandparenthood. It may not have happened on Christmas Day but was celebrated.

There were dramas and turmoils of varying kinds as I am sure there are in most families. They were resolved in one way or another and life moved on. The days, weeks, months and years were full to the hilt with work, entertaining, house guests, sport — either as participants or spectators, travel, family gatherings and bushwalking to which we became aficionados after David joined the Inaugural Great North Walk from Sydney to Newcastle in 1988.

In a note from a kindly friend prior to marriage, the following appeared:

> "Gemini with Sagittarius — What a restless entertaining and varied combination this can be. Gemini is self-contained enough to allow Sagittarius the necessary freedom and independence. Both are volatile but adaptable and periods apart can benefit both parties and strengthen the bonds."

This was probably a good synopsis of what eventuated. It did not take us long to recognise that separate times apart were valuable for enabling us to step aside from the day to day practicalities, to leave behind our ideas on things such as parenting and reflect on the things themselves. Whatever is in the stars, the Bible says that we who are strong ought to bear the infirmities of the weak and not please ourselves. The medicos say that we should let obstructive thoughts float away, while recognising that it is no more than the thought and that we need not be bluffed into giving it attention. If only it were so easy. In 1982, David wrote: "I am not the person you used to know and neither are you the person I used to know. But I would like to think that behind the understanding that is and should be generated by our experiences together that we can determine mutually what course may better lie ahead."

On 11 June 1994, David passed away in his own bed with the midday sun streaming in on him, with me holding one hand and James the other. He was diagnosed with pancreatic head cancer on 23 November 1993 and was given a stent to clear the biliary duct and stop him from being jaundiced. He was advised that a renewal of the stent might be available every three months for as long as possible. We all then went into palliative mode and David, in his own inimitable fashion, set about packing into whatever was left as much of his past that he could. He managed the leg of the Federation Walk from Sydney to Melbourne — from Thredbo to Mt Hotham over four weeks — and came straight back for a new stent only to be informed that it was now impossible to change the stent. We took off for as many luxury outings as we possibly could, went blackberry picking and jam making, entertained as many of his longstanding friends as possible and organised as much of his and my future as he possibly could. He did not manage to find me a 45 year old multi-millionaire, but kept saying he was trying. When he started talking about how much I would need for a wake, I decided that we should have a party instead and we invited about 130 people to an open house which, when people realised what it was all about turned into the most incredible event. The night before the party, he had turned yellow again. Just before the party and on his 71st birthday, he came home from hospital knowing the end was near. Two palliative care nurses arrived to meet the patient and see what was needed. David came down the stairs in his best fitting suit, greeted the nurses with his usual charm and then said "I'm off to lunch. She (gesturing towards me) will look after you". He had a group of friends with whom he always had a birthday lunch and was not going to miss it. I think it is probably what is called getting the priorities right. The palliative care nurses were just wonderful as was our own GP who travelled halfway across Sydney to visit, when he had the time after surgery, with the car full of the kids doing homework and a pregnant wife. David lasted two weeks; he was visited by half of the town; he never complained and only went on to morphine a couple of days before the end. He invited the minister from our church to visit and set about directing his memorial service. It was a grand event and I only hope he could have enjoyed it as much as the congregation did.

James and I set about the rest of our lives as best we could. James was living at home, having decided at the end of the previous year that college life was no longer for him. He finished the year with a BA in European Studies from Sydney University and set out for an honours year in Government. He was Secretary of the University Union and lined up for President for the following year. It was a great delight to his father to know that he had connections to his own university and in such a defining role. I spent a considerable amount of time after the funeral inventorying David's papers and writings and sorting things as one must. We posted just on 300 thankyou notes. Life went on.

Things less romantic

There were along the way things far less romantic a couple of which spring to mind: the recently widowed fellow student who proposed over dinner the night before he left to return to England and a male barrister who visited me in Chambers in Sydney and announced that he had just voted me the person he would most like to run away with … and was wondering when might be convenient.

In 2003 I came across *Rules for my guidance as a wife* promulgated by Isabel Burton in 1860 and to be found in "*A Rage to Live*" — A Biography of Richard and Isabel Burton by Mary S Lovell, and wondered how much of those guidelines were reflected in the letters written during our affair of the mind and how relevant they might be today if engagement in courtship, marriage and partnerships was less hasty and more considered:

"Let your husband find in you a companion, friend and adviser and confidante that he may miss nothing at home; and let him find in the wife what he and many other men fancy is only to be found in a mistress, that he may seek nothing out of his home.

1. Be a careful nurse when he is ailing.
2. Make his home snug. If it be ever so poor and small there can always be a certain chic about it. Men are always ashamed of a poverty stricken home and therefore prefer the club. Attend to his creature comforts; allow smoking or anything else, for if you do not, somebody else will. Make it cheerful and attractive and draw relations and intimates about him and the style of society that suits him, marking who real

friends are and who are not.

3. Improve and educate yourself in every way that you may enter into his pursuits and keep pace with the times that he may not weary of you.
4. Be prepared at any moment to follow him at an hour's notice and rough it like a man.
5. Do not try to hide your affection from him, but let him see and feel it in every action. Observe a certain amount of reserve and delicacy before him; keep up the honeymoon romance, whether at home or in the desert. At the same time do not make prudish bothers, which only disgust and are not true modesty. Do not make the mistake of neglecting your personal appearance, but try to look well and dress well to please his eye.
6. Perpetually work up his interest with the world … let him feel when he goes away, but he leaves a second self in charge … so that if he is obliged to leave you behind, he may have nothing of anxiety on his mind. Take an interest in everything that interests him … and if that is only planting turnips … try to understand turnips.
7. Never confide your domestic affairs to your female friends.
8. Hide his faults from everyone and back him up through every difficulty and trouble.
9. Never permit anyone to speak disrespectfully of him before you. Never permit anyone to tell you anything about him, especially of misconduct with regard to other women. Never hurt his feelings by a rude jest or remark. Never answer when he finds fault and never reproach him when he is in the wrong, especially when he tells you of it, nor take advantage of him when he is angry; and always keep his heart up when he has made a failure.
10. Keep all your disagreements for your own room and never let others find them out.
11. Never ask him not to do anything, for instance, with regard to visiting other women or anyone you particularly dislike; trust him and tell him everything except other person's secrets.
12. Do not bother him with religious talk; be religious yourself and give

good example, take life seriously and earnestly … do all that you can for him without his knowing it and let your life be something that will win mercy from God for him.

13. Cultivate your own good health, spirits and nerves to counteract his (nature) and enable you to carry out your mission.

14. Never open his letters, nor appear inquisitive about anything he does not volunteer to tell you. Never interfere between him and his family. Encourage their being with him and treat them in every respect as if they were your own.

15. Keep everything going and let nothing be at a standstill: nothing would weary him like stagnation."

It could just as easily be titled *Rules for my guidance as a husband* or *Rules for my guidance as a partner.*

THE COURIER-MAIL SATURDAY JAN. 23 1971 13

MR. David Boddam-Whetham, of Sydney, and his bride, formerly Miss Naida Haxton, of Toowong, leaving the Toowong Presbyterian Church, after their wedding last night. A cream chiffon ensemble was worn by Mrs. Boddam-Whetham, a Brisbane barrister. The wedding was followed by a reception at the bride's Toowong home. The couple will live in Sydney.

With brothers on wedding day — l to r Jim, Harry and David.

Family gathering 1985 — Bin with first grandchild.

5. Things Peripatetic

Things Peripatetic — Why travel — Childhood holidays — Family holidays — Trips, travel and tours — Travel with a purpose — Philosophy of travel

Why are we peripatetic? Why are we, who are not indigenous Australians, given to walking about or moving about from place to place? Why do we trip, travel and tour?

In 1962 I acquired a second-hand copy of RL Stevenson's *Travels with a Donkey.* In the dedication to his friend Sidney Colvin he says "… but we are all travellers in what John Bunyan calls the wilderness of this world — all, too, travellers with a donkey; and the best that we find in our travels is an honest friend". On reflection much of my travelling time has been in what was prior thereto an unknown wilderness of the world — and much of it has been in good, honest, friendly company. But however enjoyable it might have been in its simplicity and quiet reflective ways the modern world with its constant clarion call for progress has it seems made a simple trip around the countryside or wherever a far more complex exercise and one even to be philosophised about. In November 2011, after much tripping, travelling and touring on my part, I am flicking through a University of

Sydney continuing education program and discover an un-resistible course on *The Philosophy of Travel.*

In lecture No 1 of 8, I am introduced to a myriad of reasons why we travel, what we get out of it, who and what are the travellers, how and why do we travel, what motivates us to travel, why did guide books evolve, what are the ways in which people conceive of travel and enough temptation to see the course out. The range of and approaches to the topics were exceedingly broad, taking into its scope:

- ancient and pre-ancient tourism, the Greeks, the Romans and the ancient Grand Tour and what some great thinkers of the era thought about what the experience of travel could do to a person;
- the European pilgrimage in the Middle Ages, with emphasis on the importance of relics and with particular reference to pilgrimages to shrines at Canterbury, Jerusalem and Santiago de Compostela;
- the grand tour as education examining its itinerary and purpose within European society and the philosophers of the time such as Voltaire and James Boswell and what they wrote about the grand tour;
- Thomas Cook, the holidaymaker, and the introduction of most modern mass tourism as a form of social salvation;
- the golden age of tourism involving planes, trains and automobiles, especially the early influence of railways, before moving on to cruise liners and the impact of technology on all aspects of travel;
- post-war tourism with the impact of World War II on tourism in Europe and the democratisation of travel that followed with emphasis on relaxation and education;
- modern tourism and the problem of self with emphasis on backpacking, the proliferation of travel books and the existential problem of modern tourism, particularly the notion of ourselves being the thing from which we want a holiday.

I came away from the exercise much enlightened, much intrigued, much more widely read than I would have anticipated on the topic with the simple conclusion perhaps that the experience of the world, in whatever way it occurs, is part of a complete education. Jill Hamilton in her book — *Thomas Cook — The Holidaymaker* (at 82) — encapsulates the exercise very neatly: "... travel — what does it amount to? [It] provides food for the mind, it contributes to the strength and enjoyment of the intellect; it helps to pull men out of the mire and pollution of old, corrupt customs; it promotes a feeling of universal brotherhood; it accelerates the march of peace, virtue and love — it also contributes to the health of the body, by relaxation from the toil and invigoration of the physical powers".

Childhood and early holidays

Growing up in Cleveland and surrounding areas was like a perpetual holiday with the beach nearby and wide-open spaces for us to explore and play in all the time. We did not have a car in which to take trips for travel around the area and consequently any holidays we had as children seem to be with relatives. My older brother Jim and I went by train on a couple of occasions to Pomona near Gympie to a dairy farm where we learned to ride horses and milk cows and enjoyed the company of our distant cousins. We also took a train trip to Dalby to stay with my aunt and uncle on their wheat property at Dandine on the Darling Downs where one interesting, and perhaps useful, thing we did learn was how to cope with a mouse plague. I also recall a holiday I had with my cousin Claire on a dairy property outside Lismore in New South Wales where I learned that eating tomatoes for breakfast, dinner and tea would eventually give one hives. I have never been game to test the theory again.

While single, education and holiday jobs seemed to dominate to a point where lengthy holidays were not part of the scenery. I made short trips in and out of Brisbane to stay with friends at Mermaid Beach or, for rest and recreation after work had begun, I frequented Binna Burra in the Lamington Mountains where the walking was therapeutic, the food basic and healthy and the air clear and clean.

In 1963 Lesley Power (McCann) and I travelled to Daintree in North Queensland in her VW with a tarp for shelter attached to the front and rear of the VW and a metho stove for cooking. Before leaving, my mother presented me with pink shortie pyjamas with the comment, "I want you to look respectable when you get attacked". We jointly kept a running diary in a DUX exercise book, the cover of which shows "School — East Coast Motoring, Grade — Primary and Subject — Camping and lots of things". We were new to camping and had many strange and uncomfortable nights. We had a policy of staying where there were families and when desperate shouted ourselves to a caravan or cabin. Some of the highlights included being personally conducted around the Moura Coal mine; swimming at Airlie Beach, Bowen, Arcadia on Magnetic Island, Green Island, Ellis Beach, Crystal Falls; buttered freshly picked corn cobs at Atherton; staying with another Somerville House boarder, Janet Sherwin, in Townsville on the way up and the way down with access to laundry facilities; trip to Heron Island with some wonderful swimming and beaching and early morning turtle tagging. We had an amazing three weeks despite its lack of sophistication.

Over Christmas and New Year in 1966-67 I went to Malaysia to visit my school friend Sue Tan and her family and have talked about this trip in ***Things Culinary***.

Family holidays and travel

Once married, and especially after James arrived in 1974, holidays were erratic, spontaneous, and often revolved around visiting relatives or friends and often involved taking along young friends of James to keep him company. In 1975, we were at Tangalooma on Moreton Island enjoying the fishing and the weather and bringing back to me memories of a trip to the whale station that I visited on a zoology excursion when I was in high school. In 1977, we were back in Brisbane for a few days stopping over at Binna Burra on the way home: in 1978, Port Stephens and Shoal Bay: in 1979, at Barrington Tops, walking and playing tennis and later at Mount Victoria in the Blue Mountains in timber cabins from whence we did a lot of walking and played a lot of parlour games at night. In 1980, we were successful in a ballot for the first of three trips we were to make to Sussex Inlet where the Harbord Diggers Club maintained holiday cabins. It was 1980 when, on an Easter visit to friends on a beautiful property near Boorowa, I was bitten by a red-back spider who had nested in the bed I occupied. This episode has caused me to inspect very carefully any bed that is not my own before getting into it. We make several trips backwards and forwards to Brisbane and Melbourne for weddings of family friends and relatives across the years, sometimes adding diversionary rest and recreation along the way. In 1981, David and I, with James, did a return bus trip to "The Centre" from Sydney to Alice Springs via Mildura, Wilpena Pound, Port Augusta, Coober Pedy, Ayers Rock, a flight over the Olgas and an overnight at Ross River Homestead before boarding the Ghan to Adelaide and trains to Melbourne and Sydney. There were trips combined with physical activities such as golf at Bowral and walking at Barrington

Tops, Sussex Inlet, Bundanoon, Toowoon Bay, Terrigal and Norfolk Island. There is an unforgettable trip to the Gold Coast for a surprise 60th birthday party where we needed to be escorted by police around the floodwaters near Byron Bay and where, having had to keep the windscreen wipers on all the way from Sydney to the Gold Coast, decided to come back via the New England Highway only to find that it was raining the whole way home. There never seems to be anything very predictable about weather in Australia when you set out on a holiday. In 1989, David and I, with a group of his friends, made a trip from Sydney to Alice Springs, Ayers Rock Darwin, Kakadu, Kununurra, Broome, Perth and back to Sydney by plane.

1983 was the first year since 1966-67, when I went to Malaysia that I travelled overseas and it was to UK with David and son James. We went again in 1985 to Europe and UK. Here I found another world of things to learn about and do. What a treasure trove. Sometime after returning friends talked about a trip they had done to the Cambridge Summer School and what a great experience it had been. I tucked that away in my list of things to do one day.

Trips, travels and tours
Cambridge, London and Paris

It was 1993 when my aged sister-in-law wished to make a farewell trip to England to see her cousins that I went to Cambridge. She had also decided that if she was going to Cambridge to see her cousin Edith Whetham (renowned agricultural economist and Cambridge identity) that she would like to do a course on Restoration History, at the Summer School, because of the family connection to some of the signatories on the death warrant for Charles I. I agreed to go with her and set about looking at courses I could do. I chose moral and modern philosophy and the History of the English Country House. Outside the lecture rooms there were endless associated delights. Several Nobel Prize winners discussed matters relating to Cambridge Minds at the 8.30 am plenary sessions; there were evening concerts — Bach in Corpus Christi Chapel, a European quartet in Trinity Chapel, Faust dramatised in the forecourt to one of the colleges, name now forgotten — and on it went. There were early morning walks around the town with its little streets and lanes and very old buildings and trips across to Grantchester to the garden court bearing the sign "Welcome to 1910" at the gate, with yesterday's tea trays still on tables. And there were unexpected pleasures over lunch: Edith Whetham, with the privilege of being the first female member of the Schools Club, introduced us to its hallowed halls and any other place she deemed interesting, including local pubs. You never knew who you might meet over lunch in Selwyn Hall: the gentleman who asked me what I thought of the weather and when I replied (rather rudely in retrospect) that I had not come half way round the world to talk about the weather, started a conversation which lasted for nearly two hours on how life was changing, how social history was taking a different direction and how he had just completed a book on the *History of Europe*. That felt more like Cambridge.

Cambridge was full of interesting things to do and provided a great education in many areas. Then we went to London and visited Bloomsbury, the Galleries, the Houses of Parliament and the Victoria and Albert Museum (V&A). As I walked around the Museum I kept meeting this sign that said "Summer School this way". Another thing to **do** and immediately put on to the wish list with all the information I could get from Administration.

So after a short trip exhausting myself walking around Paris and Fontainebleau, I returned to London for a couple of nights with Bob Banner, formerly of Queensland debating times and his wife, Janice, before heading back to Sydney. My reading list on return included: anything from the Bloomsbury group: anything on architecture and art; anything on Bess of Hardwick; Hugh McKay — *Why don't people listen*? With the comment "… is advertising unsuccessful nagging?" I also discovered the lecture series at the Art Gallery of NSW and subscribed to anything on at weekends that might interest me.

In November 1993 David was diagnosed with pancreatic cancer and was advised that it was terminal. He died at home in June 1994. We had planned to go to Alaska this year. I calculate that I devoted about 25 hours a week to being married and needed to fill those hours, so set about using up some of those hours in travel.

New Zealand, London and France

In 1996 I am in New Zealand conducting a seminar on Law Reporting, with a side trip around the South Island.

In 1997 I take an apartment in South Kensington around the corner from the V&A, having enrolled in a three-week Summer School on Art and Architecture of the West. Then it was off to the south of France for a quick visit to parents of two French exchange students I had housed at various times. I arrived at Nimes at midnight to be met by a history addict who then took me on a tour of ancient Nimes for two hours — all lit up fortunately. Here were many of the things I had just encountered in London and could put a name to and many connections later to be made on other trips. Back to London to be greeted by what seemed to be thousands of people with sleeping bags and bunches of flowers and just in time for the funeral of Princess Diana and unprecedented security at the airport. I buy *The Sportswriter* by Richard Ford to read on the way home and follow it at home with the *Art of Decoration* by Nina Campbell and *Writing a Play* by Steven Gooch.

Alaska

In 1998 I finally make it to Alaska alone. I am met at Sydney airport by the nominated guide who announces that five persons are not enough to justify a guide and would I take the tickets and vouchers. How to become a tour guide in two minutes! Apart from me, the group consisted of a lovely English couple who had promised themselves a trip to Alaska some 50 years earlier and two sisters who were senior academics in Sydney and Canberra and refused to pay or contribute to tipping because "we don't do it in Australia". No amount of discussion about being a guest in a country where tipping was the normal part of the economy could dissuade them from their point of view. What an interesting job a tour guide has. The trip was, however, well organised and there were loads of well-informed guides along the way. I did learn that the Americans are exceedingly good at imparting information in a useful way and producing the most informative and interesting museums. I also learned that they could not come to grips with a person travelling alone and kept asking "where is your partner?". I was even asked if I would give up my allocated window seat for a couple so they could sit together on a 30 minute flight over the glaciers. From the first day in Ketchikan with a motor cruise around local pristine areas to another motor cruiser with overnights on land from Ketchikan to Juneau, there were endless new things to see and do: fishing towns, petroglyphs, the first sighting of a brown bear, nosing up close to a calving glacier, whales, seals, the odd cruise ship, a Scandinavian evening at the Sons of Norway Hall in Petersberg, the university at Juneau and a flight to Anchorage with the sun out over the coastal glaciers, then Fairbanks. Fairbanks is memorable for the overnight transformation of the town with the arrival of the pantechnicon full of hanging baskets and tubs of flowers from the "lower 49" and the flight into the Arctic Circle for supper at Fort Yukon arriving back at Fairbanks at midnight with the setting sun. From there we went to Denali National Park on the McKinley Explorer. And I went hiking after an hour of films and induction into how to behave with bears and moose, et al, and an inspection of my pack. So wearing David's Gore-Tex, I set off alone with directions and a large stick to use for making a noise to ward off predators. I found the beaver's nest to which I had been given directions, crossed snow patches and used the stick to ward off what turned out to be later identified as a Goss Hawk who thought I was too close to her nest. No bears or moose thank goodness, but I did sing a few hymns along the trail as encouragement to keep them at bay. On the following day we went by retired school bus out to the snowline in the Park, watching a brown bear stalk a moose with two calves (one for the bear and one for the moose, we were told) and extraordinary panoramas. The last day was more walking with sprouting wildflowers and a little white water rafting. It was my luck to be dunked along with the Australian guide in the icy water. But America to the rescue with a quick trip back to accommodation and strict instructions on how to have a warm bath and report in before bed. Finally back to Anchorage and a feast of the museums and Alaskan history.

I notice that I was borrowing books on Alaska — *Leaving Alaska* by Grant Sims, *Alaska- Yukon Handbook* and lots of material on water colour painting. I had enrolled in a WEA course on water colour painting which was something I had always wanted to do. My drawing was not so good so there were classes on drawing on the right side of the brain, drawing with pastels and drawing trees. The missing 25 hours a week was being very well filled with learning new things and hopefully acquiring new skills.

Cyprus, Lebanon, Syria Jordon

1999 saw me heading to the Middle East with Pamela Davenport, Ancient History teacher at Somerville House, taking students from Somerville House along with some parents and others. Here was the opportunity to see in reality what I had seen on the screen at the V&A and in preliminary readings. What a wonderful way to travel — with an experienced teacher who did annual archaeological digs at Paphos and enthusiastic inquiring young minds keen to absorb everything. In retrospect to have travelled through Cyprus, Lebanon, Syria and Jordan at a time when it was safe to do so and to have seen ancient sites many of which have now been completely or partially destroyed is a trip to be treasured. To have walked around Tyre, Sidon, Tripoli, Beirut, old Damascus, the street called Straight, Aleppo, and the Souks, Baalbek, Palmyra, Hama, a full day in Petra, the hieroglyphs of Wadi Rum, often with very few others around, are very special memories. All those glimpses into the past added to the feast of knowledge.

I had prepared myself with books such as *Crusader — By Horse to Jerusalem* by Tim Severin, *Ancient Cyprus by* Veronica Tatton-Brown, *Come tell me how you live* by Agatha Christie, which told stories of how Agatha and husband Max lived on the various dig sites in Syria, *The Gates of Damascus* by Lieve Joris and *Journey into Cyprus* by Colin Thorburn, the story of a 700 mile walk around the sites on Cyprus with a mixture of myth, history and personal anecdote, all good introductions to the area. I am still pursuing things corporate and ethical such as *Rethinking the Future,* edited by Rowan Gibson, detailing interviews with the likes of Charles Handy (with whose ideas I have always felt an affinity) and others and propounding views form every possible direction.

Paris, Spain and London

2000 was the year that I headed to Paris for the wedding of my goddaughter, Tan Lay Koon, the daughter of my dear deceased friend Sue Tan, where I was to stand in for her mother at her wedding. What an enormous honour that was. There were four days of celebrations highlighted by a father-in-law's dinner at a restaurant on the South Bank which started at 9:30 pm and from which we arrived home at 3 am, and a Chinese tea ceremony at 8:30 in the morning in the hotel where gifts were exchanged — Lay Koon's father giving her Sue's jewellery — and all of us partaking of Chinese tea from a tea set brought from the home area of the Chinese-Malay family in China. The celebrations were completed with a reception at the Le Prè Catelan in the Bois de Boulogne.

With very little time to plan I decided to take a seat on a bus tour of the highlights of Spain, a place which suggested it would add to my historical and archaeological knowledge of the Mediterranean. I arrived in Madrid and spent three days pottering around on my own, visiting the art galleries and museums and spending a full day and a half in the Prado. Again it was a place where I had an unexpected conversation with a delightful young man who was an architect from Switzerland. We shared the same nook in the dining room and found we had a lot of interests in common. From there to Barcelona which had hosted the Olympic Games in 1992 and, as the Olympic Games were about to take place in Sydney Australia, we were taken to visit the Olympic complex. From Barcelona to Valencia, Valencia to Granada and Granada to Seville, where two delightful days were spent investigating the town and the area. Seville certainly deserves its reputation as one of the most charming cities in Spain. A quick return trip to Madrid and a flight back to London to stay at Wimbledon for a few days before returning to Australia. Having had a taste for Islamic art and architecture, I returned to find as many books on associated topics as I possibly could and to educate myself a little more in this area.

Perth to Albany, North Island of New Zealand

In 2001 I tucked a trip from Perth to Albany and back to Perth on to a law reporting meeting in Perth, on which son James joined me. In August I went to Kangaroo Island by bus with my cousin Eve Abbey and in spring I tucked the Floriade in Canberra onto another meeting in Canberra.

In 2002 I ran a seminar on law reporting in Wellington, New Zealand and added to that visit a solo trip around the North Island of New Zealand.

Tuscany, Zurich and Egypt

In October 2002, having decided that I should add Egypt to my list, I spent eight weeks attending a course on Egyptian life, health and medicine, diet and food production, childhood and education, and hairstyles, writing, the role of women, economic conditions, marriage and children, childbirth, shopping and selling merchandise, burial and afterlife, the role of the wife in royalty, civil activity and trade, pottery, trade and foreign relations in ancient Egypt, crime and punishment, the Valley of the Kings, pygmies and dwarfs, pets, papyrus, etc, etc. What a wonderful introductory approach to an education on Egypt. The trip was a guided tour with an archaeologist from Sydney University. It was for two weeks only. So before I met the group in Cairo, I had been invited to stay with the French family, with whom my son had done an exchange in 1990-1991 coming home with a perfect French accent, in an Italian villa outside Cortona in Tuscany. Despite having done French to second year at university I had never had the opportunity of speaking French in a French atmosphere. However, my hosts suggested that it would be useful to have some Italian as one of the reasons that they were in Italy was to keep up their Italian. And so I had prepared myself a little by attending Saturday morning classes on Italian for travellers. Having successfully negotiated my way from Rome to Arezzo using my Italian, I found myself at the villa with six French people. Despite some very odd conversations in three or four languages at once, we all managed to have a most enjoyable time. The villa was attached to a large farm with lemonerie — not an orangerie — grapevines and fruit trees, especially those with ripening figs, all of which were available for the taking. Mornings were spent deciding what we would pick for breakfast. Lunch was often food acquired at one of the local villages and consumed on the terrace with several bottles of wine. After a leisurely afternoon we would depart to one of the little mediaeval villages in the area and then return for a very late evening dinner. There were trips to Siena, Lake Trasimene and a number of visits to Cortona which was literally just up the hill. At the Museum of the Diocese of Cortona there is the most beautiful picture I think I have ever seen — *The Annunciation* 1436 — a wood painting by Beato Angelico of *Gabriel and the Virgin*. On a quiet, wet afternoon I devoured a beautifully illustrated book on the villas of Tuscany, *Civilisations des Villas Tuscanes*, which I located in the small library in my bed-sitting room. While I had had a very happy and pleasant time it was very tiring listening to French and Italian all the time. Although I understood most of it and tried both languages, the responses were far too quick most of the time. Before leaving I was presented with a bill for a share of food, tickets purchased and a space left blank for "participation for rent". While I had not had to organise any of the stay or pay for transport to any of the places we visited I was rather surprised that it hadn't been discussed earlier. Perhaps that is the way of the French/Italians.

From Arezzo I travelled by train to Florence and on to Zürich where I was met by goddaughter, Lay Koon. A little time was spent acclimatising myself with Zürich, visiting St Gallen to see the amazing Abbey Library of St Gall and then an overnight trip to Ascona. Here we dined on mouth-watering rabbit and oxtail soup. After breakfast next day we took a walk up the mountain with magnificent views over Lake Lugano, followed by the acquisition of biscotti which, I was informed, were an autumnal event and probably the best available in Italy. What an interesting exercise in order to buy some almond biscuits. From Zürich I travel by plane to Dubai and then on to Cairo, where I meet the other travellers for the tour around Egypt.

I surmise that the trip to Egypt followed a route followed by many tours. We were however indulged by having the knowledge and experience of Dr Bourke from the University of Sydney archaeological department. Unfortunately our Egyptian guide, Hartem, was very much afraid that Dr Bourke might give us the wrong kind of information and was constantly keeping an ear and eye out for any discussions that we might have without his presence. We began with an exploration of the Giza Plateau and a full day excursion to Memphis and Saqqara before departing for Alexandria. On the way to Alexandria we visited the Wadi Natrun. On arrival in Alexandria we visited the Greco-Roman museum and amphitheatre, catacombs and the Quayet Bey Fortress, on many such occasions having the places visited to ourselves which was rather luxurious. One evening I went for a long walk by myself around the Presidential Palace and stopped to chat to a couple of families having their family day together in the same way they might do in Sydney. They had large fishing lines and were catching baby tiddlers "for the children". One family was keen to know whether the weather was better in Sydney or Alexandria. Another evening we dined at a restaurant on the Corniche where apparently Farouk had dined. On leaving Alexandria by bus to return through the estuary to Cairo for a flight to Luxor, we were provided with an armed mobile escort which changed from town to town and which was prone to keep its sirens on thus drawing attention to us as foreign visitors. On board was an Armani suited man with a serious looking gun under his jacket. At each exchange of escort there was a time delay during which we could observe from the bus that there was a deal of negotiation going on as to the amount of baksheesh to be paid. It was usually popped into someone's pocket before we could leave. How interesting the actual matter of travelling can become, how different it can be from country to country and how important to have some forewarning if possible.

Thence to Luxor, Karnack, Nefertiti's tombs, Valley of Nobles, Deir el Medina and Medinet Habu, Valley of the Kings and the Temple of Hatshepsut before joining a boat cruise up the Nile towards Nubai. The concept of these boats could only be English, the furniture and fittings having all the relish of the past combined with fabulous service and quite good food. Whilst on the boat we visited Edfu, the Island of Philae, and the Ptolemaic temples. There were a couple of very early morning starts in an endeavour to get tickets to the newly restored tomb of Nefertari in which endeavours we succeeded on the second morning. Here the colours and drawings were beautifully restored and preserved and in such good condition we were told because the tomb was filled with rubble and silt for so long; silt seems to be a good preserver of monuments in this desert country. Every location we visited seemed to get better than the last, although the 45° heat was a little hard to handle for very exposed walks such as they were. Life on-board was very pleasant, entertaining and the river itself and the surrounding landscape were endlessly interesting to watch. The chef made particularly beautiful falafels and obliged by giving us all a lesson: green beans, garlic and onion being the main ingredients. As we approached Aswan early in the morning we passed under another replica of the Anzac Bridge in Sydney; they seem to pop up all over the place. A final night on board was celebrated with a grand dinner and entertainment consisting of whirling dervishes, belly dancers and Nubian funny men.

On leaving the boat a few of us went to Abu Simbel flying over Lake Nasser, which from the air is very, very, very large. The ancient sites at Abu Simbel were amazing as was the work of reconstruction being done there. The town area was very attractively and sensibly laid out for tourists and the deviation was well worth the exercise. Thence to Crocodile Island at Aswan where we stayed for a number of days taking a camel ride to the Monastery of St Simeon one early morning. Because of my greying hair the organisers were very concerned to find me a small, gentle camel and to ensure that my ride was very well supervised. It had intrigued me along the way that every time I appeared where there were pedlars with goods for sale I was always addressed as "mother" very politely. Grey hair is something that you don't often see on the locals in Egypt. The monastery was an eye-opener into the very basic conditions under which the monks in the sixth century lived. On return to Aswan one of the group and I decided to walk to the Coptic Cathedral of St Mark in Aswan to have a look at the cathedral. A voluntary guide, a Coptic Christian, took us on a very informative tour of the church. On leaving the church we were rather intrigued to see greater activity than usual from the Armed Forces and police with barricades and guns and much to-ing and fro-ing. It was not until we got to the dining room that somebody mentioned there had been a bombing incident in Bali involving a number of Australian people. The Egyptians were taking the protection of their tourists of all nationalities very seriously. On our last day in Aswan we took a boat to visit a Nubian village and to catch the early morning river birds. Before leaving Aswan we also visited the Nubian Museum, a new and very well-presented collection spanning some 4000 to 4500 years. Sometimes it is better to see a smaller more comprehensive collection than to see a myriad of too many things as one often does in major galleries. From Aswan to Cairo by plane, to the Papyrus Institute, to the Cairo Museum to be saturated with the sheer volume of materials to be admired and by which to be intrigued. This was followed by Coptic churches and bazaars, tea at Ashwiny (of Mahmoud literary fame) where one could literally hear the buzz of his works.

One of the greatest regrets accumulated throughout the tour was the inability to be able to read hieroglyphs. I am sure that some knowledge of hieroglyphs would have made the tour far more interesting. Imagine my delight on return to Sydney when I discovered that the woman who had given the lectures which I had attended before going to Egypt was about to start a course on Egyptian hieroglyphs. There was a small number in the class and I have to admit that I have not enjoyed a course of this nature as much as we all enjoyed that course. Unfortunately, if I was sent to Egypt today I would have to go through my paperwork and learn it all over again.

Greco Roman Southern Italy, Sicily and Malta

2003 saw me heading with great enthusiasm to Greco Roman Southern Italy, Sicily and Malta with Pamela Davenport and some more Somerville House girls, parents and friends. The tour was to start in Rome and because I was coming from Sydney while everybody else was coming from Brisbane my travel to Rome was via Bangkok and London. I arrived in Rome and so did my suitcase. I am still in wonder constantly at how one's luggage happens to turn up so efficiently wherever one wants it to be. Mind you there can be hiccups from time to time. I arrived in time to join a coach tour of the Catacombs, St Paul's Outside the Walls and churches in Trastavere. The following day was the obligatory visit to the Vatican Museum — comparable only to being tinned with sardines on the day — followed by St Peter's Basilica. Next on the itinerary was a trip to Ostia Antica which brought back to me memories of having visited it on my first trip to Europe with James back in the 1980s. There followed an early pack and start for a day in ancient Rome including the forum, the Senate, Trajan's wall, Trajan's markets, temples, the Coliseum, then the Golden House of Nero which would have been remarkable to have been seen in its original state. Thence to Naples where we visited the Archaeological Museum, and on to Pompeii, Herculaneum and Oplontis, driving the Amalfi Coast and overnighting in Paestum. Plenty of walking and eye-opening ruins. Naples was not a very pleasant place to be with rubbish, pickpockets and noisy crowds and we were pleased to be on our way to more interesting places. Next on the list was a visit to the Caves of Castellana, the ruins of Egnazia and its Museum with the Divers Tomb and beautifully restored mosaics. Sometime during the course of each day Pam Davenport would provide a talk which related to the activities of the day. I recall one early morning talk on nomenclature of places and people in Roman times. We were told that people were frequently given names which related to their physical physiognomy or capabilities. A couple of the girls looked at me and pronounced very quickly that they should call me — Short Legs — because I was forever asking them to wait for me so I could catch up. The next stop was Alberobello with its delightfully interesting Trulli (houses built in an unusual circular style with conical roofs) into one of which we were invited by a young couple doing renovations. The very small houses are whitewashed and the roofs are tiled in concentric rows of grey slate making the village a very interesting and attractive site. The next stop was at Ostuni and Lecce where we set out on an evening walking tour to observe the numerous and interesting baroque, rococo buildings and the amphitheatre in the middle of town where most of the residents were out walking, a habit known as passagiere.

From Lecce we travelled to Taranto, a large industrial city and naval port but with the most intriguing museum where lovely pieces of ancient gold jewellery and pottery were on display. We were all intrigued by the cave-like dwellings cut into the limestone cliffs at Matera and a visit to a tourist hotel under ground level which reminded one of the opal mining towns of Coober Pedy in South Australia. After transferring to a ferry at Reggio to travel to Sicily, we arrived in Taormina at a beachside hotel providing an invigorating swim in the Ionian Sea. Dinner, for a change, included fresh verdura (vegetables) which we all attacked like vultures having felt very deprived of our Australian fresh vegetables during the trip. I thought that I was the only one who would go looking for a fruit and vegetable shop whenever I was travelling with a great urge to have some carrots and celery or something like that. We are certainly well served with our fresh fruit and vegetables in Australia and it is a matter upon which many of my overseas visiting friends have commented admiringly. The first full day on Sicily was occupied by a trip up Mount Etna, at least as far as the 2003 eruption would allow us to go. The scenery was very black with bits of greenery from existing orchards, including cherries and chestnuts, being visible in the black soil. Here I acquired a box of the most beautiful cherries I think I have ever tasted which was shared around the bus with great delight. The day ended with arrival at Palermo with its magnificent Norman buildings, having stopped along the way at Cefalu to visit the cathedral and the lavatio, a 16th century wash house, with which that the students engaged quite practically. Palermo, with its Arab-Norman reminders in nearly every building — lavish marble in the church of St Giuseppe del Teatini, the bell tower and Byzantine mosaics of the medieval church, la Martovana, and the absolutely stunning interior covered with gilded mosaics of the Cathedral of Montreale. This has to be the most perfectly proportioned and decorated church ever. It included the most beautiful cloisters with Romanesque capitals, all individually different and depicting animals and plants. Of all the religious places I have visited it is the one I did not want to leave and would love to see again. A cloistered life in a place like that would be a very calming experience. Leaving Palermo with regret, we travelled to the archaeological sites at Segesta and Erice, and the Valley of the Temples on the way to Agrigento and the Ancient Roman Villa of Casale at Piazza Armenia, regarded as the eighth wonder of the world. Here one saw and experienced so much of the lavish and luxurious lifestyle of the wealthy Romans portrayed through the beautifully restored works as to understand the daily life, the original architectural structure and the typical household furnishings of a luxurious lifestyle. The mosaics and frescoes, once again preserved by centuries of being buried under soil and silt, were an ancient history education in themselves. Of note was the room with the girls in bikinis in athletic poses. Then on the way to Syracuse we stopped in Caltagirone, famous for its ceramics which are displayed especially on steps and in public places. Our last stop in Sicily was in Syracuse where the highlight was a visit to the Art Gallery to view and to introduce the group to two Caravaggio paintings — *The Interment of Santa Lucia* and the *Adoration of the Magi.*

Next stop Malta and another lifestyle and history altogether and a hotel in Valetta where the lift did not work on the night of arrival. Lessons learned at difficult times: from one of the students who kindly and efficiently carried bags up the stone stairs for many was a request of me for a lesson in packing as my case was the lightest of all. Another two Caravaggio paintings — *The Beheading of St John the Baptist* and *St Gerome* — were added to the list at St John's Cathedral on a tour of the town. One got the impression that there was nothing that could be described as typically Maltese and that the island has been shaped by historical events created by the location of the island. The visit to the island finished with visits to the Roman catacombs said to date back to the time of Paul and James, to Hagar Qim to the temples of pre-history dedicated to the Gods of fertility, to the caves of Ghar Dalam with a vast array of fossil bones and teeth belonging to dwarf elephants, hippopotamuses and deer believed to be well over 18,000 years old, when it is thought that Malta was joined to Italy — not to North Africa — and finally to the Blue Grotto.

Back to Sydney I went, via Rome and London for a few days, including the Greek and Roman Galleries at the British Museum as a top-up. To have travelled again with a group who asked why and how and when and learned so much by the answers given, the sights seen and the wisdom and knowledge of the leader, Pamela Davenport, was an education in motion.

Norway, Sweden and Copenhagen

In 2004, son James was committed to a wedding in Stockholm and thought it might be a good idea if we had a holiday together in that area before the wedding and a good idea if I found something for us to do together. Having had at some time been recommended a Hurtigruten cruise down the Norwegian coast, I made investigations and booked us on to a ferry which turned out to be the MS *Richard With*. We flew into Oslo and spent two very busy days visiting the Oslo Art Gallery, taking in the Edward Munch paintings and generally having a very good look at the town. The lilac was in full bloom and the strawberries at every corner were freshly picked. We then flew to Kirkenes where we had just on 24 hours to wander around the town, take an early morning walk visiting both the cemetery and the Grenseland Museum on the Russian border near the Finnish border. The Museum was staffed by Russians and had a very interesting collection of local art. As the Hurtigruten ferries are literally ferries and stop from time to time to load and unload passengers, load and unload goods, it was not long before we were stopping at our first town, Vargo, and before the day was out we were rounding North Cape in very nippy weather. It was not unusual to be woken in the middle of the night to find timber or cars being loaded or taken on or off the ferry. As we moved further south the weather changed, more sun was seen, and we took advantage of every opportunity to go ashore and wander around the little towns and villages. The architecture of the houses was interesting and different and the lovely muted colours with which many of them were painted were intriguing. Bridges which were often sighted in the distance were elegantly designed and constructed and, believe it or not, we ran into another replica of the Anzac Bridge in Sydney as seen earlier on the Nile in Egypt. Our hosts kept talking about the advent of spring which was not far away. We stopped at a place called Bronnoysund, where the spring flowers were freshly out and full of colour. It was a bit like being in Alaska and suddenly finding that there were flowers everywhere except these were actually in the ground. Most of our time was spent in the viewing lounge or walking around the decks. The scenery, the constant changes in weather and views kept us on the move. At Trondheim we were taken on a tour of the city and visited both the Gothic and the Nedaros Cathedrals. At Moldo our land excursion, late in the evening in daylight, was almost overrun entirely by a football crowd all heading in the same direction. We disembarked at Bergen for another two days of wandering round and enjoying the scenery, the cathedrals, the home of Edward Grieg and the eco-friendly lodge in which we stayed.

We then took the fast train from Bergen to Oslo admiring the beautiful lush countryside along the way, being committed to get off the train at certain stations to admire the view of the snow in the mountains, and finally arrived in Oslo to find that the only accommodation for the night was on a ship moored in the harbour. It was the most unusual accommodation I think in which I have ever stayed and, as there was a theatre on board, it was not very quiet or very comfortable. The train trip to Stockholm was in contrast quiet, comfortable and provided glorious views of the green farmland of the interior of Sweden with its rust-red houses and barns and the odd field of yellow canola breaking the varying greens. James's youthful optimism that we could find a hotel for me at the station paid off with a hotel called the Lady Hamilton in the old town which was a delightful, helpful and friendly place to stay. He, along with other wedding guests, was booked into a former gaol in the middle of a river but now a youth hostel. From the Lady Hamilton, with its maritime decorative theme, I spent the better part of four days walking around the city on foot-aching cobblestones, going to museums, royal palaces, the oldest theatre in the world at Drottingholms Slott, using the public transport, visiting public buildings and, most interesting of all, spending half a day at the Vasa Museet, where the museum is devoted entirely to the ship *Vasa*, its building, sinking, recovery and restoration. I even managed an exhibition of Georg Jensen which, of course, epitomises the classic design of the Scandinavians. A most amazing place! It was here in Stockholm that James and I, missing our vegetables, one morning went to a supermarket and found celery and carrot which we ate in the adjoining park. I asked at the hotel one day where I could find a traditional Swedish dinner and was directed to a local restaurant where I had a dinner consisting of dried meat fried with potatoes and onions and beetroot on the side. A very unusual and, it seemed to me, not very healthy meal after all the beautiful salads and things that I had been able to find in city Stockholm.

After four days of wedding events in and around Stockholm it was time for us to part company; James to Sydney and me to a few days in Copenhagen. One of the great treats in life is to have an adult child without any appendices completely to oneself for a time. We learned a deal about each other's likes and dislikes and habits and enjoyed the conversations over dinner, on board and on land. It is a memorable and treasured time.

First up, I managed to fit in a three hour tour of Copenhagen including the Changing of the Guard at Amelienborg Palace and the Constellation where the cruise liners berth. Afterwards it was to the National Museum telling the history of Denmark in a clever and well-designed layout. The next day was a bus to Rosenberg Slott for which I was required to buy two tickets as the tickets were only sold in pairs. Shades of Alaska! In the palace museum there was a magnificent display of royal jewels and gowns, some going back over many centuries and, across the road, the National Art Gallery. Another day finishes with feet aching from cobblestones. On the last morning a visit to the Glypotech Museum produced a large and varied Etruscan collection together with a fabulous collection of famous French master painters. In the afternoon the Tivoli Gardens (a must I had been told). Not so sure that a large collection of restaurants was a must see place. Then another bus ride which passed through wealthy scenic areas along the coast, this time to Helsinore Castle, the Summer Palace and Frederiksberg National Historic Museum in another magnificent castle. The day ended boarding the plane for home.

French Alps and Turkey

Having been unable to go to Turkey with Pamela Davenport, I had added it to the list and, in 2005, the Archaeology Department of the Australian National University was offering a study tour of Turkey in September — *From Mother Goddess to Gallipoli: An Archaeological Odyssey in Turkey.*

There was time to visit another classmate from Somerville House on the way after an eventful departure from Sydney which was pre-empted because of a light coming on in the cockpit and had consequences in departure at Hong Kong. Here there was insufficient time for the transfer of my luggage but not of me. On arrival in Zürich I was immediately notified of the absence of my luggage and promised that it would be delivered from Vienna to the address that I was visiting in the French Alps, where it duly was two days later at 7am. So with backpack and handbag I trained it to Lausanne where Roslyn Young was waiting for me and we drove to the tiny village of Bouclans, with its glorious hanging baskets of begonia and fuchsias, etc. Here I spent five very hospitable and most enjoyable days taking part in the rituals of life in another country and in another person's home. Ros went to France in the 1970s and became a renowned expert in teacher training and language teaching. An opportunity to practise my very poor French was quickly dismissed with the request: "Naida, can we talk in English as I feel I am getting behind with my colloquialisms?" Ros also had a theory that one could talk more in the car and talk we did while running around the local areas visiting many of the famous tourist attractions. Not only did we talk in the car but we talked over meals on extraordinary topics such as thought processes, world trends in spirituality and teaching methods. To have one of the world's big thinkers to oneself for even a short time was a great treat for me and a great gift from her. Our first stop was Besançon where Ros had spent most of her teaching career. The Musee de Beaux Artes housed a most interesting archaeological collection from beneath the town and surrounding areas. Later we visited Beaune to see Les Hospices de Beaune which was used in fact as a hospital until the 1970s. On the same day we visited Les Plus Grande Caves de Bourgogne where we were taken on a wine-tasting tour of the collection which contained some four million plus bottles of wine. Other talking trips included a drive through the Jura Mountains along and around the rivers Doub and Saone through the most spectacular green forests and valleys; a trip to Alsace to the town of Colmar with its incredible collection of early Renaissance religious art and local archaeological treasures at the Musee d'Unterlinden. We travelled home via the back roads driving through famous Riesling vineyards noting the millions of semitrailers from every point in Europe and Asia which travelled through France in one direction or the other. What an amazing logistical exercise that must be! Before leaving there was a visit to the local village and a walk to the forest where I was never out of hearing of bells on cows and sheep, met a horse, found some delicious wild raspberries and had a little feast. With a very early start I then took off via Lausanne and Zürich to Istanbul and from Istanbul to Ankara.

Described as a study tour, the tour of Turkey was designed to provide a basic understanding of the cultural structure and development of this fascinating country derived from past and present history in a manner that could be described as fun or enjoyment in execution. It commenced at the Museum of Anatolian Civilisations in Ankara with displays of spectacular collections from the Neolithic, Bronze and Iron Age times. This was followed by a visit to the Byzantine Citadel, the Haci Bayram Mosque, which is built among the ruins of the Roman temple of Augustus and Rome, and to the Ataturk Mausoleum. The following day was spent in and around the Hittite capital of Hattusas and the various surrounding sites. Then it was a drive through central Anatolia to Cappadocia with the fantastic landscape of pink and white "fairy chimneys", which are in fact pinnacles of eroded volcanic ash, and visits to as many significant sites in and around Goreme and surrounding areas that could be reached. After descending into Peristema Gorge, we took a long walk to inspect the preserved Byzantine churches with their beautiful frescoes. We followed this with a visit to a strange little town on a hillside to see the source of obsidian. Here there was a wedding, taking place with lots of varied costumes and dancing, to which we were all invited. People in Turkey seemed to be very friendly indeed. We then crossed the Konya Plain visiting one of the most important Neolithic sites in the world. We arrived in time for an evening's entertainment by an important mediaeval Whirling Dervish group. We then crossed the Taurus Mountains visiting the cities of Perge and Aspendos on our way to joining our yacht at the Finike Harbour for a trip along the Aegean Sea to visit some of the wonders of classical civilisation. Our host on board was David Price Williams, an archaeologist, who: had worked on classical sites all over the Middle East including Syria, Jordan, Lebanon and Egypt; had lectured at the Institute of Archaeology for the University of London and was a Fellow of the Royal Geographical Society. David held us mesmerised with his interest in keeping us well fed and watered and with his knowledge and flair for imparting it — a long pre-dinner talk on the topic of the Mediterranean Sea, a recital from Aeschylus in the Roman theatre at Myra and poetry whenever the occasion seemed to warrant it. There were many trips to shore by rubber dinghy for visits: to extraordinary sites; to private homes of tomato farmers for lunch and breakfast; to the island of Kekova to visit the sunken city; to explore and compare Roman, Hellenistic and Byzantine relics and sites, Ottoman remains and a Lycian Necropolis. For sheer delight and enjoyment was the afternoon when the sun was out, the wind was right and the sails went up to the sound of the 1492 overture as we travelled up the Aegean coast. With some reluctance we left the boat at Gocek and boarded the bus that would eventually take us to Istanbul. Along the way we visited the sacred site of Didyma to see the still substantially intact gigantic oracular temple to Apollo, Miletus and Selcuk. From here we visited among other places Ephesus, the remains of ancient Sardis, the ancient acropolis of Pergamon, Troy and Cannakale from whence we crossed the Dardanelles for a full day at Gallipoli. Our last days were spent by bus, ferry and foot in a flurry of visits to the famous attractions of Istanbul, including the Agia Sophia, the Blue Mosque and the Topkapi Museum. As a study tour it certainly provided a good way to get to know the complex historical connections, the different cultures as well as experience the variable and regional social habits.

Chicago, Washington, Philadelphia, New York, Paris and London

In 2006 I was invited to a birthday party in Paris and what I did on the way was to go on a NSW Art Gallery Society tour taking in the art and architecture of North American cities, they being Chicago, Washington, Philadelphia and New York. There were only 20 of us and two guides, who in America were, we learned, titled "docents", a word I had never encountered before but readily added to my vocabulary. As I had never been to the lower 49th at all it was a fascinating experience. We all fell in love with Chicago which was so clean and beautifully presented with the streets full of flowers and happy people. We spent a lot of time looking at architecture, art and anything and everything to do with Frank Lloyd Wright. I caught up with Mary Maher, one of my research assistants from law reporting days who had a four-month-old baby and we spent a very pleasant afternoon together. In free time I found a huge and most amazing collection of stained-glass windows at the Smith Museum on the Pier — a place that was not advertised anywhere, nor for which was there any paper information to take away.

We arrived in Washington on an incredibly hot afternoon to be taken on a tour of the monumental highlights. One could spend weeks at the Smithsonian Institute in all its various incarnations. We were very lucky to have extraordinarily clever guidance at all of the places we visited and to have very good accommodation as well, which made things a lot easier. In Washington we actually stayed at the Sofitel Hotel, which was very luxurious and central. The cultural attaché to the Australian Ambassador put on a cocktail party for us. There was an Australian opera singer for entertainment adjacent to a then current exhibition of Australian Aboriginal paintings. We went to a new play called *Shear Madness* set in a hairdressing salon. This play had been running for some 37 years and varied its ending according to the way the audience voted at the beginning of the second half as to who had committed a murder. We laughed ourselves stupid; it was very, very good light entertainment.

Philadelphia was low-key, low-rise and low in impact. What a fascinating place. We were intrigued by the architecture of the original old city; we loved the Museum of Arts and most of the people loved the shopping because it was 18% lower tax than in New York or anywhere else. We travelled out of Philadelphia to view a collection of the Barnes Foundation which contains some 180 paintings by Renoir. As you can well imagine we reached a point where we would be happy never to see another Renoir painting. Many of them were not very good.

New York is something else altogether isn't it? Of New York, loved its art, loved its architecture, loved its people and actually got to enjoy its food. I took myself to a diner for the experience and enjoyed it all. I guess one could spend months there without ever visiting all of these interesting galleries and museums but we certainly did our best in the time that we had. I spent one whole day at the MOMA where I had my photograph taken by a Japanese journalist/photographer (Chie Nishio) for use in a collage of a "mature faces" in an exhibition in 2007. That was an interesting encounter. When I asked a local why she might have chosen me out of all the people sitting in the gallery foyer, the reply was — because you have not had a face lift — thus making my face real! I saturated myself with illuminated manuscripts at the Morgan Museum and Library and generally exhausted myself getting around by foot so as not to miss seeing anything at street level. We went to another play *Avenue Q* with Jim Lyons (*Sesame Street*) and his puppets. Great theatre! The people with whom we travelled were mature, pleasant, educated, generous and very, very pleasant to be with. It was quite different to travelling on one's own. We parted after a farewell lunch at the Tavern on the Green in Central Park. It became my lot to express appreciation to the tour leaders for their contributions. The two outstanding aspects of the trip were the collections we saw — some of the world's great collections — and the connections to which we were introduced, connections to other world collections, to other artists, to our pre-existing knowledge of art and connections to other galleries able to facilitate visits at out of hour's times and so invitingly.

And then to Paris for the combined 40th birthday party of god daughter Lay Koon and husband Philippe D'Ornano held over two very glamorous and very luxurious days. I arrived hot and bothered from New York, through Heathrow, which was not the most comfortable experience, even in transit. By the end of the trip and after 12 different airports I was very good at ensuring there was nothing in my hand luggage that was offensive. I had back-packed my party gear and sufficient makeup for a couple of outings just in case my luggage did not make it. Fortunately it did. The first evening we went to a private dinner at L' Ambroisie, a restaurant in the Place des Vosges. We were welcomed to a private room and were informed that we would be expected to stay for at least four hours to go through the magnificent menu that was designed for us. It was an evening to remember. There were about 10 to 12 small degustation dishes and the most exquisite wines to go with them. No one felt there was too much food, or there was too much drink, or felt overfed. The company was great as well. Lay Koon, her husband, her father Ching Keat (CK), Philippe's parents, me and Philippe's boss and wife from New York. There was a glorious mixture of languages and ideas. We duly sat for over four hours. The next day, CK and I went to breakfast and then to the Guimet Museum of oriental arts, which had reopened after 17 years of renovations. A most engrossing and amazing collection! We then lunched at the Trocadero and prepared for the evening party at the Pavilion on the Champs Elysee. After a long leisurely lunch on the Sunday morning I headed back to London by plane. My Wimbledon friends had moved to Knightsbridge where they had a rather large apartment around the corner from Harrods. This was very convenient for all kinds of things I wanted to do and a number of things we did together as well. I met up with Janice Aylmer-Pearce, a Somerville classmate, went down to Kent overnight and spent something like 24 hours talking non-stop. I then spent the weekend with Lay Koon and Philippe, who now lived at Chelsea in London and caught up with a number of other people. It was a great luxury to be able to stay so comfortably in London.

Kimberley, Newcastle and Tasmania

Later in the year I did a 12-day bus tour from Darwin to Broome through the Kimberley with cousin Eve Abbey. In 1989, David and I had done the same route by plane (on what was then known as a Kangaroo Hop ticket) which flew us from Sydney to Perth, via Alice Springs, Darwin, Broome and Carnarvon. It was interesting to be on the ground and to see things more closely. I stayed on for a couple of days to have discussions with and to meet with and deliver some Kids HelpLine material to a contact for BoysTown.

In 2007 there was a short trip to Newcastle with Eve and another short trip to the Hunter Valley with Bev Folliot.

In November 2008 I went to Tasmania on the first of three trips for small groups that I did with Australian Eco Adventures. The trip was titled *Tasmania — the Wild Side* and focused on that island's natural areas and provided some opportunities for walking. We criss-crossed the island: from Launceston to a climb to the top of Mt Barrow then to Eddystone Lighthouse and back to Launceston; to the Western Tiers and overnight at Cradle Mountain with a very interesting walk around Dove Lake, before moving on to Smithton via Rocky Cape National Park. From Smithton we explored the north-west corner visiting Aboriginal sites, cruising the Arthur River and walking in the rainforest around Lake Chisholm. We then took to the newly opened highway linking the Tarkine Wilderness with the west coast towns of Strahan and Zeehan, exploring around Lake Macquarie by bus and boat before heading through Queenstown to enjoy bushwalks around the Franklin River and an overnight stay at Giant's Table and Cottages, where watching the resident platypus was certainly on the list. The next day started with a visit to the Gordon Dam, followed by Mt Field National Park, Russell Falls and through Bushy Park to Hobart for a couple of days locally occupied and a day trip to Bruny Island. I took advantage of an offer of a side trip to Bathurst Harbour, flying in to Melaleuca over the south-eastern corner of Tasmania, spending the day in, on and around Lake Bathurst. We visited the bird hide before boarding the plane for the trip back over forest land, much of it denuded. We were so lucky and privileged to actually see one of the few protected orange-bellied parrots still alive.

On leaving Hobart we headed to a very wet and cold day at Port Arthur which had changed somewhat since my first visit in 1972 on honeymoon. We headed north along the coast to Bicheno which provided some very pleasant walks along the shoreline with colourful rock formations. This was followed by a day of walking within Freycinet National Park dipping down from Coles Lookout to Wineglass Bay and back across to the beach on Promise Bay. As we walked and talked, we observed the roos on the beach, the after effects of fires, the remains of middens and the huge variety of mosses. Finally, back to Launceston via the historic towns of

Campbelltown and Ross and some country roads where we saw fields of opium poppies in full flower.

South East Coast of Australia

In 2009 it was *Ships, Shores and Secrets of the South East Coast* with Australian Eco Adventures, starting at Sydney, travelling down the coast to the mouth of the Snowy River and then up through the State Forests of Victoria, through Orbost, Cooma and Braidwood to Sydney. It amazed me how little we actually know of the history of our own back yard, when leader Ross Dixon set about introducing us to the Aboriginal significance of many sights, the history of early European settlement along the coast, the progress and demise of the whaling industry, the trials of the early timber/cedar-getters, the still important fishing industry, the sea transport between ports and bays, the history of the Jervis Bay Nature Reserve, now known as Booderee National Park, where and why the early settlers chose to go, where convict labour was employed, the advent of lighthouses to protect coastal shipping, the life of isolation by its keepers and families, the development of sawmilling, shipbuilding and farming, the Moruya River quarry for the Sydney Harbour bridge pylons, the gold rush at Tilba, the scenery of the Sapphire Coast with its beaches, swans, whales and other natural delights, game fishing from Bermagui and cheeses from Bega, the Benboyd National Park and the natural beauty of Mimosa Rocks National Park with its endangered sooty owl and golden-tipped bat, the important wetlands maintaining the ecosystems of the lakes and lagoons providing habitat and food for a range of waterbirds (both local and migratory), the solution to the difficulties of crossing the sand bar at the mouth of the Snowy River and, finally, Cooma developed as a significant town through the local farming, grazing, mining, timber-getting and tourism. It was a physically beautiful trip and a mind-enhancing experience in sympathetic company.

Eyre Peninsula, the Bight and the South-West

In September 2010 it was my third trip with Australian Eco Adventures, this time covering the *Eyre Peninsula, the Bight and the South-West*, billed as 17 days of exploring coast and hinterland and areas of South Australia and Western Australia — whales, wildflowers, wineries and wonderful coastal and rural scenery. The highlights included, once again: the small size of the group; exploring historic and beautiful Eyre Peninsula; crossing the famous Limestone Plain that is the Nullarbor; following and watching whale history and whales; being overwhelmed with spectacular wildflowers, forests and coastal scenery; being introduced to amazing National Parks; cruising in the Archipelago of the Recherché; walking to the south-western tip of Australia in the Leeuwin Naturalistic National Park and much, much more. Every day seemed to bring a new experience and a new delight.

From Sydney to Port Augusta via Renmark, a highlight for me was a visit to the Bishops Lodge in Hay. This is a remarkable iron building constructed in 1889 as the official residence of the Anglican Bishop of Riverina. The house has a beautiful 19th century garden planted with an acclaimed collection of heritage roses. It features advanced technology in design and construction to counteract the harsh climate of the area and original paintwork on the exterior corrugated iron walls and on the zinc coated tinplate interior walls. Aspects of the design and building features could surely be usable in some of today's architectural wonders. At Port Augusta, another highlight was an introduction to the wildflowers at the Australian Arid Lands Botanic Gardens and the reasons why arid zone plants have evolved in special ways to collect and hold water and to have thick waterproof skins to reduce evaporation. The introduction was extremely relevant and valuable as we crossed the Bight. Apart from Whyalla, which I had visited on a couple of occasions for BoysTown, everything until we reached Albany was completely new to me. Eyre Peninsula boasts some of the largest commercial fisheries and shellfish harvesting in Australia, of which we were delighted to partake, as well as agricultural products. From here on we were overwhelmed by the prolific wildlife, especially birds, including sea eagles, ospreys, oystercatchers, gulls and dotterels, with pigeons, parrots, kestrels, eagles and emus in other places. A visit to Port Lincoln National Park, covering much of the size and tip of the peninsula, was enhanced by a private tour by the owner of the only private National Park in the area. Leaving the Eyre Peninsula via Ceduna and Eucla, we began our crossing of the limestone plain of the Nullarbor, visiting the Head of the Bight to observe the Southern Right Whales on their annual visit for calving. From Eucla to Esperance we explored cliffside lookouts, telegraph stations, jetties, beaches and the Cocklebiddy Caves.

Our stay at Esperance was long enough to enable us to explore the isolated beaches, headlands and heathland of Cape Le Grand and Cape Arid National Parks and to appreciate the expert attendance of a local wildflower expert who seemed to know exactly where to take us to find the most interesting and beautiful of wildflowers. With the sun fully out we were also able to walk along beaches and headlands in a very relaxing manner, with cameras at the ready all the time. Leaving Esperance we followed the coast to Hopetoun, then the Fitzgerald River National Park and into the Sterling Ranges before arriving at Albany on King George's Sound. Here we began with a visit to the historic features such as the port, the old jail, churches and the spectacular coastline with a diversion to see the large karri and tingle trees of the Valley of Giants in Walpole. From Walpole we boarded a wilderness cruise to the Nuyts Wilderness Peninsula and then to Pemberton through the lush grazing country and forests to reach the coast at Leeuwin for a walk to the lighthouse before making an overnight stop at Busselton. Before arriving in Perth to head home we visited Mandurah, the industrial centre of Kwinana, Fremantle with its historic buildings and waterfront pubs and cafes and did an orientation tour of Perth and Kings Park.

Once again the Eco Adventure had lived up to its expectations. Information was provided and questions answered in a most obliging, intelligent and informative way; almost without exception the trip was visually beautiful or overwhelmingly spectacular; people we met and places we visited provided extraordinary hospitality and kindnesses. My most treasured possum jacket, which I dropped without realising at Leeuwin Lighthouse, was returned to me in the post by the park ranger who had picked it up. Good things happen from time to time and this trip was certainly full of good things happening.

London, French Alps, South East England

By 2010, I feel the need to slow down, spend more time in one place and take time to enjoy the company of friends. Lay Koon and Philippe have acquired a daughter, Zoe, yet to be met. I head to Bob and Janice in Knightsbridge in London in May, from where I go to Ros Young in France for a few days. Once more we are in a car where the conversation flows freely and in English. We head for Guédelon at Yonne in Burgundy where a team of 50 odd people have taken on an extraordinary feat of building a castle using the same techniques and materials used in the Middle Ages and estimated to take about 25 years to complete. We spend the day immersing ourselves in the various different phrases of the castle's construction. My children's books, which I acquired at the National Gallery in London while doing the art and architecture course at the V&A Museum London, come to life with full force and effect. I return to London to potter around, finally making

John Sloan Museum and spending a weekend in Kent with Janice Aylmer-Pearce and her husband, Bowen, visiting local places not seen before. I then move into a studio in Chelsea close to Lay Koon and in between meeting daughter Zoe and spending time with the family I spend a weekend with my English penfriend with whom I have been corresponding since the age of 12 and had previously met in England. She and her husband live at Southend-on-Sea in Essex and treated me to a lovely day at Hyde Hall the home of the Royal Horticultural Society near Chelmsford. On the way home via Singapore I hop across to Johor Bahru in Malaysia to spend three nights with Lay Koon's father, Ching Keat, little knowing that it would be the last time that I would see him alive.

Tasmania

When I left BoysTown after 10 years of service in late 2013 I was gifted an Art of Nature three day trip to Tasmania including MONA, Friendly Beaches Lodge at Freycinet and a day with Peter Adams at his property *Windgrove* on Roaring Beaches where sculpture and landscape become one. I went on this trip in early 2014. It was a whirlwind tour of contrasts, beauty, magnificent Tasmanian food and wine and delightful company. On arrival at MONA we were taken on a private tour of the gallery, followed by wine tasting and dinner where we had the dining room and the chef to ourselves. The apartments are named after Australian architects and artists and I spent the night ensconced in a magnificent unit overlooking the water named after Arthur Boyd. There were original paintings of his on the walls. Day two we travelled along the east coast to Friendly Beaches Lodge, an environmentally sustainable lodge, hidden in a private sanctuary and surrounded by stunning Freycinet National Park. The time was spent walking the beaches and some of the local walking tracks, swimming and enjoying once again delicious meals with produce from local areas. An early morning walk along the beach without another person in sight created some very special moments. Day three we headed down the east coast to *Windgrove* on the Tasman Peninsula where Peter Adams hosted us on a tour of the property upon which he has spent many years planting some 8000 trees and creating several large-scale Earth Art sculptures. My co-workers at BoysTown explained that they thought it would combine my love of art with my love of walking. It certainly did.

London and California

In 2010 I acquire my first grandson, Claude, and being a grandmother becomes another very regular part of my life. In 2012 Auguste (Augie) is born and, in 2014, the family move to Walnut Creek in California in connection with James's business. Consequently it is not until 2014 that I return to London once again to catch up with friends and to join a mini 55 year class reunion luncheon in London. I take another studio apartment in Chelsea from where I simply potter around spending time revisiting places I have enjoyed such as the Wallace Collection, the V&A Museum, and the Physic Gardens at Chelsea. I catch up with Lay Koon and her family and with her brother Loh Koon and his family. I go from London to Walnut Creek in California where I spend just over two weeks enjoying the company of my own family. I return to California for a month in 2015 for another visit. On this visit I actually get to see a little of California as James and I and the boys spend a couple of days driving through the Napa Valley and visiting cousins outside Sacramento. It is almost time to think about another trip to visit people rather than places.

We are all different. We all travel, trip and tour. We all have our own reasons for doing so. We all have our own memories of these expeditions both good and bad but life would be less enjoyable and less memorable without. They certainly provide plenty of good "food for the mind" and help nurture the body.

With brother Jim on a holiday with cousins on a dairy farm outside Pomona in Queensland.

On a Roman road outside Besançon in France.

2004 June — Somewhere in the Arctic Circle with Horseman Mt in the background.

Wrangell in Alaska inspecting petroglyphs.

On Mt Etna carrying a bag of locally grown cherries.

Turkey — on the Aegean Sea — Flash VI awaiting our return from some ancient site.

Mother on a safe camel in the Egyptian desert.

Accommodation from the ridiculous (Queensland 1965) to the sublime (Paris 2007)

6. Things Fraternal

Things Fraternal — Friendship — How, when and why — Being a Neighbour — Befriending — Reunions — Alumni — Staying in touch — Philosophy of friendship

On our way through life we enter into friendships in many ways — as children, as teenagers, as adults, at school, at university, at work, within families, in love, socially, in communities, playing sport, relocating, travelling and, apparently, on the Internet. Somewhere in life we meet, we connect and sometimes we stay connected whatever time or space or distance has separated us. We reconnect with conversations that were left off 10 years ago, two years ago or yesterday as if they had been continuing all along. Where do the most treasured relationships come from and why do they last? Some friendships are fleeting, some are long-lasting and many remain connected for life. Why do we hit it off with some people and not with others? Has it something to do with having the same moral background? My husband described our initial relationship as an affair of the mind. Perhaps friendly relationships are all affairs of the mind. Perhaps they are allied to moral philosophy. Are they a necessary part of living? It was Aristotle who stated that "Friendship is a kind of excellence … and necessary for living". Has it morphed into something quite different in the Internet "era of instant, push-button connectedness"? Why do some friendships survive on mutual help and kindness and others are so complete as to require no such considerations?

Primary school connections

So I go back to the person with whom I have had the longest friendship to date — Helen Withers/Burdett. I met Helen as a five-year-old in Stanthorpe. We went to the same Sunday school and school, we played after school at each other's homes and then the family left Stanthorpe for New Zealand from whence my father had come. When I arrived at Somerville House in 1956 who should be in my class but Helen and we reconnected from day one and were boarders together for one year and we have continued to reconnect ever since.

At the age of six in Auckland I meet for the first time my 16-year-old cousin, Evelyn (Eve) Holden. As young children we were very daunted by the sight of her glass eye in a jar in the bathroom. She turned up in Brisbane many years later and then when I came to Sydney resurfaced at Manly as Eve Abbey. Eve has spent most of her life involved in bookselling in Sydney — Abbeys Bookshop, Penguin Book Shop, Language Book Centre, Galaxy Bookshop and Henry Lawson's Bookshop — and for many years a judge on the prestigious Miles Franklin Prize. We share a love of books and reading: we have travelled together to Penang in Malaysia, Queensland and the Sunshine Coast, to Kangaroo Island, to Broome, to New Zealand for a family gathering; we have subscribed to concerts together. We now share many a weekend meal where Eve provides one course and I take the other. We talk books and recipes and TV programs and much that is topical, and each visit is over far too quickly.

On our return to Australia after several months of very wet weather from which my mother insisted we come back to where the sun shone we settled in Cleveland, outside Brisbane. Here I completed my primary education at the local state school and it was here that I met Margaret Power. There is one memory which relates to Margaret and me and which I cannot erase: we would spend an afternoon after school 10 to 15 feet up a custard-apple tree, helping ourselves to custard-apples the size of footballs and reading our dictionaries. I have a vague idea that there was a race to finish but as Margaret had a small OED and I had a very ancient dictionary (which I still have falling apart at the seams) it was probably not very evenly balanced, but that did not matter. Margaret's father died very suddenly and she disappeared out of my life to reappear again in Sydney where she was lecturing in Economics at the Sydney University, and from which she has retired for a life as a yoga therapist. We haven't taken up reading dictionaries together but we have taken up long stimulating and interesting conversations over a meal or on the telephone. There were many "girlfriends" at primary school, two Gwendas, an Elaine, a Marlene and my cousin, Claire, who lived not far away. When we all headed off to different secondary schools these friendships were, as might be expected, more transitory than long lived.

At the age of 12 I acquired an English penfriend as was the popular activity of the time. Today I guess it would be a Facebook friend! We have followed each other through careers as a hairdresser and a lawyer, marriage, and children growing up and the acquisition of grandchildren. I have every letter she has written to me in my mother's hatbox where special things are now kept. I have never been able to convince Janet and her husband, David, to come to Australia but they have been more than hospitable on several visits to them in Essex. On the last occasion in 2010 they introduced me to the Royal Horticultural Gardens at Chelmsford. I would miss the exchange of news each Christmas.

Somerville House connections

For me it was an all girls' high school which my mother chose so I would find out what girls did, having been raised with three boys, having learnt to bowl overarm and play tennis with a cricket bat. We had to wait till our 10th birthday to get a tennis racquet and brother Jim needed someone to play with at home. Here I met up again with Helen from Stanthorpe. As a boarder I made some very long-lasting friendships. There was Tan Suan Cheng (Sue Tan) from Malaysia: we corresponded, I visited and I became Godmother to daughter Lay Koon. Sue died when Lay Koon was 16 and when Lay Koon married I was honoured to be asked to stand in for her mother. Lay Koon is more than a friend. Despite the physical distances between us the relationship exists somewhere very close to that of mother and daughter. I am Aunty Naida to all the family and relatives. There was Lesley Power (McCann): in 1965 Lesley and I travelled to Daintree in North Queensland in her VW with a tarp for shelter and a metho stove for cooking. We had an amazing three weeks despite our inexperience in the camping side of things. I supported Lesley at her marriage to Barry. However irregularly we meet the threads of the last conversation are picked up, recipes and herbal remedies are exchanged and discussed; we walk and talk together; we lament becoming grandmothers at an age where the body is not as willing as the soul. In more recent years there is Sally Staines (Philp): widowhood deeply cemented a previous sporadic connection when her husband, Russell, died some years ago from the same insidious cancer as my husband; Sally comes from a background of cattle grazing and I became the co-driver on trips to Taroom in Queensland where she had inherited a property, *Yeovil,* and where we embraced a totally different lifestyle for weeks at a time; in Sydney we speak almost daily and share theatre tickets and bushwalking days. There was Karin Abt (van Schyndel) with whom I share a birth date. For over 50 years, there have been two birthday cards which have come and gone each December with a note that simply says *2013 from Karin* or *2014 from Naida*; we catch up with news in the Christmas card. Just after Christmas 2006 James tells me that he has met a girl at a dinner party whom he has taken out a couple of times. He says that they have "decided that they come from the same moral background". Her name is Nicole Goldschmidt. Surprise of surprises, her mother is another classmate from Somerville House. Brenda Bryan (Goldschmidt) and I once passed an athletics relay baton to each other on the Brisbane Cricket Ground back in the 1950s. Brenda and I now have a friendship that grows with our grandsons, Claude and Auguste.

As I did not live in Brisbane itself I had little time with daily travelling to make too many friends among the daygirls. However, the parents of Kathy Martin (Sullivan AM) welcomed me into their home for overnight stays whenever I could not get a train home to Cleveland and we remain friends to this day: we debated together after leaving school; we shared many experiences including balls and outings; I was able to return hospitality when Kathy was Senator for Queensland and one of the few women in Federal Parliament and called upon to attend functions interstate; Kathy was responsible for introducing me to BoysTown. How Janice Noble (Aylmer-Pearce) and I became friends is obscure but may have had something to do with being banned from a school activity for misbehaviour in class. Jan was sent home and I was sent to the boarding school hospital for the afternoon. We stayed buddies through university and throughout her travels overseas after both her parents had died. I would periodically receive a string of numbered aerograms and parcels in my mail from somewhere on the overland route from Bombay to London. When Jan decided to stay in England and marry, her aunt and I sorted and dispatched her stored belongings: Bob Banner stood in for me at Jan's wedding in London when I could not make it; she comes to Sydney; her daughter becomes my surrogate daughter for three years while studying in Sydney; we Skype; I go to London and Kent where we meet, reminisce and potter around as though it was yesterday.

When we finish senior year, we agree to meet 10 years out at 10 am on the 10th day of the 10th month beneath the GPO clock in Queen Street, Brisbane. Over 40 girls turn up and we reunion thereafter every five years. Throughout that process others become friends for lunch, for visits, for travel. They include Beverley Gardam (Folliot), Heather Simpson (Professor Thompson) and Catherine Prentice (Dr Smith OANZ) in New Zealand, Susan Russell (Dr Bambrick OBE), Roslyn Young who was awarded the Palmes Académiques in France in 2001 for services to education and Penny Stevens (Doherty) to name but a few. There is a very real pleasure, that is hard to beat, in seeing each other and carrying on those half-finished sentences left somewhere in the past. I have been involved in planning the reunions for many years and enjoy the regular reconnecting with familiar faces.

When married and living in Sydney, Patricia Aaron (Barkell) from a class above me but in the same school house turns up living around the corner and pregnant with twins. Our lives become intertwined: we shared baby minding; we took the children out together; we did knitwit sewing classes together; travelled to western Sydney to acquire knit fabrics by weight and had sewing days; we socialised; Jim, her husband, briefed me at the Bar; Patricia moved back to Brisbane with the children and we catch up from time to time and, when she becomes terminally ill with cancer, I am forever grateful to BoysTown that I am in Brisbane so regularly that I can visit her.

University and beyond

University and college living provide more opportunities for forming friendships outside Somerville. At Milton House I meet up with women from different areas of Queensland who are doing a variety of different courses. Some I stay in touch with, others resurface when least expected. At university there are so many more students and so many more things to do and, by the time I start Articles, there is not much time for forming long-term relationships. However, the most enduring relationship at this time comes out of the decision by Kathy Martin and me to join Young Liberals in order to debate. We teamed up with one Robert Banner; we got on together and continued to debate together for a number of years. Bob was doing accounting while working in a firm of accountants. Bob was always happy to escort me to events when I required a partner and I was happy to partner him on similar occasions. Bob topped the accounting exams for the Institute of Chartered Accountants in Australia and was offered a position in the United Kingdom. When his boss invited him to a private dinner party to farewell him I was very pleased to be able to accompany him. Unfortunately, to my embarrassment, and to some loss of the enjoyment of the occasion I was violently ill during the course of the evening, an embarrassment never to be forgotten. When Bob took off by boat to England Kathy and I turned up at the dock to farewell him with a bottle of champagne, cheese and biscuits. We did not think to take glasses and implements and ended up drinking the champagne out of the bathroom glasses in the cabin and cutting the cheese with a nail file which I happened to have in my handbag. There then began a continuing correspondence ranging across a very eclectic mix of topics. In 1972 I received a letter with a photo of the newly acquired Siamese cat with the comment "apart from getting married she [the cat] is the principal event since last writing". It took a couple of letters to find out that the name of the wife was Janice. Janice, I later discovered, knew me as "N", the strange woman who wrote to Bob signing off thus, and whose letters were kept filed chronologically. Janice and I sorted ourselves out late one night in the kitchen at Wimbledon over a bottle of sherry. In February 1975 they arrived on our doorstop in Sydney following a disastrous visit to Bob's family in Brisbane, with son Nicholas, a few months older than James. As Bob wrote on his return to England: "It is really people not places that make the most impact". This seemed to become the pattern of our continuing relationship: letters, visits to and from; we stayed with them, David stayed with them, James stayed with them, I stayed with them; they came to Sydney to watch the fireworks on New Year's Eve; Nicholas came to stay over New Year, arriving quite ill with shingles, having spent time surrounded by chicken pox in Brisbane, before heading to Cambridge. James and Nicholas, at time of writing, are both living and working in the USA. I only hope we are not growing too old to travel so far to catch up with each other. Bob and Janice were also people with a caring and giving morality. Janice ran an annual Fashion Show in Wimbledon in aid of good causes and persuaded the ladies to devote one year's show to a mental health charity then called the National Schizophrenia Fellowship, now Rethink. Bob was de facto treasurer for the event which bought him into contact with the Rethink staff and, eventually, an invitation to join their Board as Treasurer, then Chairman, leaving a larger and financially much stronger charity. While doing this he discovered an associated trust company of which he became and remains Chairman, tidied up its governance and managed its sixfold growth over fifteen years. As a result of the preceding he was awarded an OBE in the final year of chairmanship of the charity.

Work provides a different atmosphere. Ailsa Heathwood, who had been an articled clerk at Flower and Hart and admitted as a solicitor in 1957, returned from a stint overseas during my articles and became involved with training the clerks. We eventually became and stayed friends both in Brisbane and then Sydney. And, without any designs in that direction, Ailsa was instrumental in introducing me to the man I would marry years later.

I met Ian Gzell at university, like me doing Arts/Law. Ian married Sylvia Butts, who had been at Somerville. I joined the Queensland Bar and a set of chambers with Ian from whom I learned many valuable and practical life skills related surprisingly to accounting — it started with keeping the petty cash balanced. I babysat for them when they were stuck. They watched the Brisbane Head of the River from my unit. Ian and Sylvia come to Sydney in the late 1980s and we take up where we left off. We continue to share conversations, meals, recipes and books.

There were other and more fleeting friendships. On a rest and recreation stay at Binna Burra in the Lamington Mountains I met a simply wonderful English lady of 70 years with sensitivity and "quality" and a belief in the honest use of words, of whom I wrote in 1969:

Today

I said goodbye — au revoir — I hope

To a friend

Acquired so easily

Yet so fleetingly;

Age has no meaning, but what we put into it ourselves.

To be able to meet her again

On her home ground

"The Steps" — near Uckfield in Surrey, England.

So very far away in distance and age but so close in reality and thought.

I am sad for the parting ...

We connected and stayed in contact for years. She came back to see family in Brisbane; we wrote to each other and sadly her family wrote one day to say she had passed away.

Once in practice I found friendships in those around me, some of whom are still in my life, such as the Hon Ian Gzell, the Hon Robert Hulme, who moved my admission in NSW and marked the brief , "One bottle of Scotch", David Jackson QC and Francis Douglas QC. Ian and David and anyone else in Chambers at the Inns of Court in Brisbane on Saturday mornings, including me, would often adjourn to Milano's restaurant for a late lunch and frequently leave by the back door when discussions on all sorts of topics had passed the normal closing time. Des Draydon was one who befriended me with advice, help, briefs and lifts and, as I have said elsewhere, endeavoured in practical ways to take some of the naivety out of me. He always acted with propriety and good common sense. He loved driving and when we went to Canberra for the Inter-Varsity moots in 1965 he insisted on driving the whole way himself. We arrived in just over 10 hours!!

Another person whose exact entry into my life I cannot recall was Jean Russell (McCulloch). I think perhaps she briefed me: she certainly continued to do so. Jean started life with the law as a stenographer and had the wonderful facility of being able to take shorthand at remarkable speed. She was admitted as a solicitor a month after I was admitted to the Bar. We began by meeting for lunch and then discovered we had much in common in terms of lifestyle: we liked cooking and sewing and talking law. We took ourselves to a sewing course at Helena Kaye, which was a Brisbane dress shop that produced the most beautiful linen outfits. Here we learned to make patterns, cut fabric correctly and do the most intricate finishes, including rouleau and beading. Jean had a house at Mermaid Beach and we often spent weekends there sewing and gardening as well as enjoying the beach atmosphere. When Jean married Bill McCulloch, I helped to make her going-away outfit in blue linen with a heavily beaded pocket on one side. Jean had two children quite late in life, ran a suburban practice and later did locum work throughout Queensland. Her talents were multi-faceted and skilled. I last saw her in about 2004 at Burpengary to where she and Bill had retired.

Sydney

When I married and came to Sydney I acquired two wonderful sisters-in-law in Vincentia (Vincie) Anderson and Madge Boddam-Whetham (B-W), both steady and practical. With them came nephews, Hartley and David, who are always there in very supportive ways. Both married exotic women, Pamela and Jeanetta, who needed to be inducted into the ways of the Aussie world and we grew together in transferring that information. Extended family relationships have a shape of their own which seems to be very malleable when families expand. They are more fraternal or brotherly in nature by virtue of kinship or how they connect. There is what Wordsworth described as a bond of "common feelings of fraternal love" that maintains them.

We first lived at Fairlight near Manly and became friendly with some of our neighbours, sharing meals and activities. Jan and Lance Grant were near neighbours with young children. When they decided to start a cherry orchard outside Mudgee, David took to helping with great enthusiasm and a box of cherries arrived around Christmas for a number of years. We stay in touch by telephone and the odd visit but the connections are still very much there.

When James started at Mosman Prep School he became friends with a David Howard. David joined us for holidays and outings and James loved going to the Howard home where there were older brothers. David's mother, Mary, became a friend with whom I went to aqua rhythmics and school functions. We decided that David liked coming to our place for the peace and quiet and James loved going to their place for the boisterous activities. When we moved to live on the other side of Spit Bridge, these friendships dissipated somewhat. There is a strange phenomenon about bridges in Sydney to which I was introduced early in my living here. Sydney people do not like "going over the bridge" for anything not absolutely necessary. James and family met up with David and family in California early in 2015 and they apparently discussed why Mary and I had "stopped being friends" concluding, I am told, that crossing the bridge had something to do with it. Friendships may well have suffered on that ground. If it did, it is regretful.

David Eager was best man at our wedding and had a valuable understanding of the B-W psyche. His daughter, Harriet, worked for me as a research assistant in the mid-1990s. We all understand each other and stay connected at Belvoir Theatre and vegetarian dinners. Harriet has bravely agreed to help James out if I go bonkers. I have noted in ***Things Legal*** the continuing sporadic friendships with those who worked with me at the Council of Law Reporting.

I met Beatrice Gray at the Sydney Bar in 1973 as I have recalled in ***Things Legal***. In retrospect it was an instant and binding meeting of minds, interests and intellect. We were in practice together. We had our first child a few months apart. We took some time out and spent time pushing prams around talking furiously and getting to know each other. We have been meeting and talking ever since. We are in almost daily contact one way or another on topics ranging from the legal principles in the latest High Court decision to the cut of Julia Gillard's jackets. I introduced Beatrice to Law Reporting which became another constant topic of conversation. We can still spend ages on the phone discussing a recent judgment in the High Court or the Supreme Court of NSW. Some 30 years ago we started taking the other to long lunches for our birthdays and continue to do so today. The original idea was to go somewhere we had never been before. We have started to go back to places we really liked. We occasionally go to theatre or concerts together. We shared the experiences of having husbands with terminal cancer, of family dilemmas and weddings of sons. If, as Aristotle believed, "Friendship is a kind of excellence … and necessary for living" then our friendship is certainly that.

Next-door to me in chambers in Macquarie Street was a clinical practitioner, Jennifer Braithwaite, whose door opened and shut mysteriously throughout the day. We chatted when we saw each other for long enough. In the course of one chat she introduced me to a very useful concept — that a large percentage of people are dysfunctional but do not wear a label telling us so. I went through a stage of being beleaguered by people who wanted me to solve their personal problems. I was reminded of something I had read in *The Courage to be yourself — A Woman's Guide to Growing Beyond Emotional Dependence* by Sue Paton Thode, where I had noted with some affinity in the content of Ch. 9 — "Drowning in life's debris is like being a responsibility sponge. When we assume responsibility for other's happiness we become everybody's designated garbage can or doormat … dump here". Jennifer's one-line advice was to respond by asking "what are

you going to do about it?" It is some of the best advice I ever had and has proved more than useful on many occasions. We were on the same thought level and are still pursuing all kinds of topics.

With the project to digitalise the law reports for the Council of Law Reporting for NSW in the mid-1990s (detailed in ***Things Legal***) Margaret Calvert entered my life as the Council's solicitor. Margaret acted for me when I litigated with a publisher over personal copyright issues. We started a friendship outside law; we went to theatre together; we met and talked; we "came from the same moral background". Margaret moved to a small holding outside Charters Towers in North Queensland. She recuperated from surgery in my spare room; she returns to Sydney at least twice a year and we go to theatre and films and walk and talk and exchange recipes and shop; I have stayed with her and her partner at *Sandalwood* and we have met up for the Chamber Music Festival in Townsville; we Skype. It is interesting how an initial relationship based on a professional lawyer/client relationship can become something more personal and rewarding when least expected. There are threads to be found in similar backgrounds which seem to be absorbed through a process akin to osmotic action.

Keeping in touch with many friends is facilitated by reunions of past connections, alumni gatherings and travel. Bushwalking friends though longstanding tend to remain just that although, on occasions, we might meet off the beaten track. There are many others who became friends by T T S-ing (Talking to Strangers). At my brother Jim's 70th birthday, his eldest son held us all enthralled with recollections of the children's embarrassment when Dad talked to strangers and had given him the title of T T S-er (Talker to Strangers). How often has it happened within families? Maybe it was genetic as all four of us were good at it. I have met many people in such a way who have come into or through my life, stayed for a while or are still here. The meeting places have been varied: on public transport, on ferries, on holidays or just walking up the street. They have all made life more interesting in one way or another. One hopes they feel the same way about such engagements.

Befriending

Dictionaries define befriend as to "become friends; to act friendly towards; to aid". Gandhi regarded the act of befriending to be the quintessence of true religion. My experience with befriending those in need, while the act may have been neighbourly in a religious or Christian sense, turned sour when others thought they saw an opportunity less worthy but more self-satisfying. Who is my neighbour?

We once had and 80 year-old, very determinedly independent neighbour, near blind himself, with a wife with Alzheimer's who frequently called out for help with something he could not manage. David helped with fixing things and gardening, I took to cooking and baking extras and taking them over. All was enthusiastically received. One day he asked me why we did these things for them. When I replied that he was my neighbour, there was nothing more, he did not seem to, or want to understand, despite having grown up in a missionary home. There was something more he wanted and it turned out to be someone who would promise to look after him for life and never to put him in a nursing home. When his wife died that person came out of the woodwork, took him over and eventually put him in a nursing home, and managed to inherit when he died. A similar history occurred with another widowed friend of many years who eschewed my assistance for similar offers of help.

There were also a couple of single women in my life who were happy to be befriended. The family of one were so intent on getting what they thought they were owed that it became impossible to advise or help with the extreme manipulation going on in the background and I felt compelled to walk away. Another on the verge of bankruptcy with a mortgagee sale happening and full breakdown on the way occupied many months of the time of both myself and another friend, collating her possessions, sorting them and dealing with creditors. Some years later a message got to me that she had told friends that I had stolen her mother's towels and did not wish to know me. I have no idea what that was about but many relationships fail or end because of regrettable misunderstandings.

Choosing friends

In a small class when undertaking a professional course, I made the acquaintance of a younger woman who made overtures for friendship. She was extremely clinical in her approach. She invited me to join her for lunch and over lunch produced a small notebook in which she indicated to me that she had made plans for her networking group of "friends". She showed me how she had divided her networking group into different categories according to how they might be useful to her. She indicated to me that she had put me in the group labelled "personal friends". I must admit that I found this approach somewhat confronting and left the luncheon wondering how on earth one could decline to be a personal friend. With very little knowledge of her personally I was dubious as to what we might have in common other than the fact that we were attending a professional course together. When she turned up in my chambers at 8am one morning shortly thereafter wanting immediate and urgent matrimonial advice, I was able to tell her that family law was not something I did and that I was unable to help her. Networking had become a very fashionable thing to talk about at the time and I did wonder why or how it might be useful in terms of making friendships. It was clear to me that what was being sought was not really friendship but a personal adviser, someone who might be useful, not even a mentor. There was no meeting of minds, interests or intellect which would have cemented a relationship. People are endlessly intriguing in the manner in which they approach many things, including socialisation.

Internet friends

Whilst I am happy to use the Internet as a mode of connecting with established friends, I could not bring myself to use it as a means of acquiring friends or maintaining the friendships I enjoy. I cannot imagine what sort of friendship would eventuate from an invitation I heard recently on the television to "friend up on Facebook". Perhaps it is an age-related view but I suspect I am not on my own. I watch people on public transport especially, smiling and chuckling as they are checking their Facebook on phones and IPads, and wonder quietly what they are getting out of it. Robin Dunbar, a University of Oxford anthropologist and psychologist is known for predicting that the number of people the average person could have in a social group is 150. In an article on *The Limits of Friendship* by Maria Konnikova in 2014 in the *New Yorker*, she uses his work to propound that networks like Facebook are changing the nature of human interaction: whilst it enables one to keep track of people, does that kind of superficial friendship, as distinct from face-to-face friendships, lack the synchronicity and sheer pleasure of face-to-face shared experiences? It might be easier to have more friends when one has Facebook, Twitter and Instagram to help one to cultivate and maintain them, but it changes the nature of human interaction and probably changes the nature of true friendship as developed, propounded, enjoyed and philosophised about for centuries. Is it just a kind of mechanical socialisation rather than friendship?

The philosophy of friendship

Friendship seems to be a topic that fits under the heading of Moral Philosophy and a topic much discussed by the early philosophers, including Plato, Aristotle, Socrates and the Stoics. It is now something that is widely discussed and not only by philosophers, ethicists and those interested in social morality. In 2005, I came upon a little book by Mark Vernon — *The Philosophy of Friendship*. It canvasses every aspect of friendship imaginable hopefully illuminating the "perils and promise of friendship": friends at work, friends and lovers, on being used, on being useful, sex and friendship, platonic friendship, civic friendship, garden friendship, politics of friendship, friendship and other relationships and spirituality of friendship. Vernon concludes "Friendship is the desire to know another and be known by them … Philosophy is not, therefore, just illuminating a friendship. The very possibility of friendship lies at the heart of philosophy. … To seek friendship is to seek wisdom". However one tries to understand friendships, why they matter and what motivates them, they are important to what I would refer to as a good life; they are about liking people for who they are, not just for what they do or what they can do for you. And when you find that person who is one who comes from a similar moral background you may find yourself with a true friend.

It is interesting to contemplate the connections between relationships and friendships. While relationships (for example same-sex marriage) are becoming institutionalised, friendship has not come to that point. Will it? It has certainly become publically socialised — perhaps oversocialised — via facilities such as Facebook. Does one really want or need one's relationships with others publicly available, discussed, liked or not liked by people known or unknown? In a contemporary setting there is such a huge variety and complexity of ideas about friendship one could be forgiven for having difficulties in finding and keeping that true friend.

Somerville House boarders' Sleepover at North Sydney -
Naida, Karin van Schyndel, Sally Philp, Helen Burdett and Lesley McCann.

Somerville classmates lunching with Roslyn Young on a visit to Brisbane —
clockwise Ann Beaty, Sally Hall, Naida, Ann Hecksher, Jenny Greenhill (decd), Bev Folliot and Ros

With cousin Eve Abbey.

With Margaret Power in 2012 at McMahons Point.

Margaret Calvert in her prolific vegetable garden on Sandalwood near Charters Towers.

A reunion of debaters in Sydney in 2004 — Robert Banner, Kathy Sullivan and husband Bob Sullivan, Naida and Janice Banner.

God daughter Lay Koon with Phillipe and Zoe, Paris 2016.

7. Things Culinary

Things Culinary — Food, glorious food — Cooking — Gardening — Fishing — Eating — Entertaining — Dinner parties — Celebration cooking — Volunteering cook — Exchanging recipes — Memorable meals

The old adage that we eat to live but do not live to eat comes frequently to mind around culinary activities. Eating should accordingly be something we do to maintain health but not become a favourite activity. Culinary activities involve food, growing food, cooking food, eating food and enjoying the associated activities.

Things culinary have been endlessly shaped and reshaped, recycled, reprocessed, reused, reinvented, rejuvenated, revamped, reclassified, documented, modernised, popularised, mediatised, Facebooked and selfied. Would the absence of any of them impair the ability to enjoy life?

Eating food has been a great occupation of all peoples through all time. Alexandre Dumas says, in his *Few Words to the Reader* in his *Dictionary of Cuisine*: "food whets the appetite in many different ways … Gluttony demands quantity … Epicurism demands quality".

Man has not always sat at table to eat, or used cutlery or table linen, or even partaken of three meals a day. I query, however, whether man needs to sit on a pavement sniffing petrol fumes as seems the wont today.

Early Mediterranean peoples first reclined to eat, used fingers and bowls for washing hands and many still do. Early cutlery was made of many different materials and in all shapes and sizes. Guests brought their own table napkins which transitioned from hay to soft bread to hanks of wool, then cloth. They have today moved on from fine linen to paper of varying quality, attractiveness and usefulness. Bibs are still offered in some seafood eateries. Is there not still something rather special about formal dining at table with fine linen, glass and crockery?

Conversation was one of the enhancements of the first great and beautiful dinners enjoyed by the Greeks. They tended to be structured conversations on set topics wherein they developed theories on such subjects as culinary and social matters. The French, according to Dumas, seem to have perfected a conversational model for all of Europe from midnight to one in the morning — "between the pear and the cheese. The conversation ranged from the great questions of the day to those of preceding centuries, and was developed at table with profundity, reason, and light, by Montesquieu [et al]".

In more modern times we had the salons where literary and philosophical topics were popular. Today conversation, unless orchestrated, has progressed to politics, gossip and real estate. I am reminded of a sister-in-law who would invite me to lunch with erudite friends and having given me the topic of conversation would add something like: "… and Naida, if they start to stray from the topic will you please say something provocative". It was indeed an interesting ploy and worked if needed. I must admit to employing a similar technique in widowhood when inviting single guests to dinner on the proviso that I would cook, but they must bring a topic of conversation and a bottle of wine. Strangely it worked best with the male of the species.

Wine first came in earthenware (some still does), goatskins (plastic casks),and, from the 14th century, glass. Spices were rare until the 17th century. Cabarets and taverns developed into eating houses and cafes and finally restaurants.

From earliest times food was celebrated in art forms, in painting, in magazines, in newspapers and cookery books. Now it is mediarised and orchestrated, almost ad nauseam, in television programs. Food, cooking and eating are now so well documented as to be overwhelming. This growth may be attributed to modern life and modern lifestyles but also to the greater variety of food that has been developed, travelling experiences with food, multiculturism and more, together with the sheer volume of information available on every topic imaginable: cooking for two, vegetarians, gluten free, vegans, invalids, elderly, infants, children, etc; cooking with: rice, pasta, quinoa, fish, beef, lamb, chicken, etc; cooking in: pots, tagines, woks, slow cookers, camp ovens; thermomixers; cooking on barbecues, open fires, etc, etc.

Growing up with food

I love food. I love growing food. I love cooking food. I love eating food. I love sharing food. I think I have always loved food although some food has not loved me.

One of my earliest memories connected to food is of helping my mother make a large bowl of green junket sprinkled with hundreds and thousands for my older brother, Jim's sixth birthday. This was devoured by a band of small people on the verandah of the house in which we then lived at Ballandean near Stanthorpe in Queensland.

This house was not far from the main interstate railway line from Brisbane to Sydney. It was near a prolific apple and pear orchard on which my father worked. In the curtilage to the railway line grew the most wonderful asparagus, which we loved to pick and cook and eat. Some 30 years after we had left the area the memories still lingered. On a sole road trip from Sydney to Brisbane via the New England Highway I stopped for a breather at Ballandean and took a walk along that railway line where the asparagus still grew. I picked as much as I could find and on arrival in Brisbane at brother David's house with the bunch in my hand was greeted with: "You stopped at Ballandean?" When we went to live not so much later in Cleveland, not far from the railway line there, we discovered some wonderful asparagus beds growing right next to the tracks. These we not only picked regularly but tended for many years. It supplemented our own home-grown spears for many meals. The soot from steam trains was obviously a great fertiliser for asparagus.

Ballandean was also the place where I was introduced to rabbit, for which I have continued to have a predilection. I can still see the rabbits hanging from the clothesline. I can still taste that rabbit wrapped in bacon and stuffed with goodies. Our father had trained as a chef at Pt Cook in Victoria when in the New Zealand Navy and my memories seem to be that, when he cooked, it was fairly memorable. I recall with great clarity a time when my mother was in hospital and he produced Scotch Eggs — something of which we had never heard and never had again as I recall. They were boiled eggs coated in something made from a tin of spam. This is not to deny my mother's skills.

But what really stimulated my interest in food and cooking was the *Children's Picture Cook Book* that my mother gave me for Xmas 1947 and which I still have.

Mind you it is somewhat the worse for having been spattered with ingredients and has a couple of pages missing. The cover, which is a very girlish pink, says:

> "recipes .... Margaret Gossett
> designed by .... Elizabeth Dauber
> William R Scott inc .... New York"

At the age of six, as I then was, I was not tall enough to work at the kitchen table and nor was my older brother Jim or my friend Deanna from next-door. Both of them were sufficiently interested to want to join in this wonderful new activity. Our parents' solution was to let us use a wooden kitchen chair as a work table and often to use a heavy saucepan as a mixing bowl. There was no such thing as an electric beater. Why a heavy saucepan? Well it was more stable than a light aluminium bowl and more robust than a glass bowl. It worked remarkably well. It was a most popular Saturday morning activity. And I recall my father complaining that he never got to eat any of the muffins we cooked because they had all been sampled by the willing neighbours, to whom we were very keen to show off our newly found culinary skills. Part of the learning process was the dreaded washing-up. It was a good lesson learned early. I am pretty sure that we tried every recipe at one time or another and some became, as the smudges still evidence, great favourites, like: the One Egg Cake; Cookies; Muffins; Ginger Snaps; French Toast; Caramels; Chocolate Fudge, which was the best recipe when it came to making fudge for canteen nights at Girl Guides years later.

The next recipe book with which I became familiar, and still am, was my mother's:

COMMON SENSE COOKERY BOOK
COMPILED BY
THE PUBLIC SCHOOL
COOKERY TEACHERS'ASSOCIATION
OF NEW SOUTH WALES
TOTAL ISSUE 216,000 COPIES
NEW AND REVISED EDITION
ANGUS & ROBERTSON LIMITED
Sydney and London

It, like my own first recipe book, is tattered, spattered and the pages have been scattered. It contains so much wonderful plain English instructions for all sorts of things that one who cooks needs to know as well as some incredible advertisements for such things as the Griffiths Collapsible Steel Frame Ironing Board — "The Strongest and Most Rigid Ironing Board Made", which "Should be in every home" — Price 19/11. But what practical and useful introductory pages containing lists of kitchen requisites, a dictionary of terms used in cooking, pictures of cows and sheep showing cuts of beef and mutton suitable for baking, boiling or grilling, timetables for cooking meats, tables of measures and lists of joints and their accompaniments! It still contains handwritten notes and additional recipes in both my father's and my mother's handwriting and newspaper cuttings of prize- winning (10/6) recipes. One of these is my mother's own recipe for Christmas pudding.

Cleveland, where I spent most of the years from six to 23, was then known as the "Salad Bowl of Brisbane". We lived on a very fertile block of land and had a well with a pump so grew nearly all our own vegetables and lots of fruit. We (and I mean everyone in the family in one way or another) planted, watered, hoed, weeded, picked, packed, sold, gave away and, most importantly, cooked and ate, radishes, parsley, carrots, beetroot, lettuces, apple cucumbers, cabbages, cauliflowers, potatoes, broccoli, chokoes, beans, peas, poor man's beans, snake beans, turnips, pumpkin, squash and kohlrabi to remember but a few. My father seemed always to have a passion for the slightly different or exotic in whatever he decided to grow and so we acquired at an early age a taste for many things not heard of today. It was not uncommon to sit down to an evening meal with four to five different vegetables on the plate. This was no inconsiderable amount for a family of six and the odd stray who was never turned away from the door. So of course we learned to pick just the right amount, to prepare, peel and cut into pieces. Mostly we steamed vegetables, in what my father always called (with a typical New Zealand accent) a "cullender". Having been a chef, he also liked to have the right sauces so, at an early age, I learned to make white sauce and mint sauce to go with the roast mutton. Mint sauce was something we children took turns in making. Such a simple recipe, needing only:

1 tablespoon chopped green mint (home-grown as well)
1 tablespoon white sugar,
1 tablespoon boiling water
1 tablespoon vinegar;

But, in retrospect, what a great way to get kids involved in the meal process other than setting tables and clearing up.

The proverbial and much maligned choko vine is probably the most prolific thing to grow anywhere. It has grown on or near to most places I have lived. I still have my mother's collection of choko recipes cut from a variety of magazines and Sunday newspapers. At various stages in my culinary life I have taken them out and used them or passed them on to friends. "Clever cooks can achieve wonders with the Choko" and "Pickle it, boil, it … you just cannot beat it" headlined a couple of paper clippings. There is pretty well nothing you cannot do with a choko: preserves, jam, chips, creamed, chutney, mock pears (coloured with cochineal), mustard pickles, moussaka, choko-fish cream curry, creamy minted choko soup, choko soup with rice, chokoes a la Polonaise, choko and tomato casserole, choko flapjacks, ratatouille, choko and zucchini salad, bread and butter chokoes, choko and corn relish, choko and lemon jam, and for dessert; chokoes and ginger and chokoes with pineapple, to name but a few of the documented recipes I still have. I have to admit to trying out many of the recipes over the years to find that they were often quite well liked. The choko and mint soup went down well in a family of soup addicts. I used to love picking the choko when very tiny to steam and eat with butter. Most people turn up their noses and are not a bit interested. Each to his own taste!

We also grew fruit, especially strawberries, raspberries, mulberries, Cape gooseberries, pawpaw, bananas, mangoes, custard-apples, guavas, passionfruit and rosellas. What we did not grow often grew along the railway line, the nature strip, in the next-door neighbour's yard or on a farm not far away. So with berries (and chokoes) in abundance and rosella bushes I became a jam maker or, at least, an assistant jam maker. The rosella flower makes the most wonderful jam but the rosella bush is rarely seen these days. I once saw it in a floral display at my dentist's rooms in Sydney in about 2007. On a return trip to Cleveland, in 1990, I stopped with great delight at nearby Ormiston for a sign on the roadside that said "Rosella Jam". The Cape gooseberry made a great jam as well. The berry was small and round and an interesting golden yellow when ripe and lived in a little paper hood, like something out of the May Gibbs Gumnut books. It was full of tiny seeds which seemed to put many people off eating it. It was a plant that was, what I would call, bird-seeded. The *Macquarie Dictionary* describes it as "a tropical solanaceous herb, *Physalis peruviana,* cultivated for its yellow edible berry, native to South America, and naturalisd in high rainfall areas of southern Africa, the east coast of Australia, and other areas of similar climate". Some bird seeded it into my terrace garden in North Sydney in the early 1990s and I suddenly remembered that it went very well in what we called in the family a pizza pie. This was a pie crust, filled with a Philly cheese and egg mixture which was baked, allowed to cool and then topped up with jelly: red jelly with strawberries; yellow jelly with gooseberries. I had made a whole string of them for No 3 stepson's 21st birthday lunch.

As far as we were concerned Cleveland could also have been known as the "Fish Pond of Brisbane". Because of the proximity to the beach and a little creek, known as Ross Creek, which entered through the mud flats (later to become a whole canal styled suburb of Raby Bay) on the other side of the railway line and opposite where we lived, seafood became part of our daily lives. Handlines were the thing. One saved the money from strawberry picking or waited for a birthday to become owner of a fishing rod or a bike or a watch or a tennis racquet. We would always take a line when we went swimming in the baths at the end of Millers Jetty or at Raby Bay. Bait was flour and water and/or bread. Sometimes a little bit of aniseed was added as enticement, though the fish were so plentiful it really did not matter. The target was garfish, but anything else that nibbled and was caught (other than jellyfish or the like) was taken home. Garfish are small and full of bones for the uninitiated. They were scaled, gutted, beheaded and put through a mincer to become, with the addition of egg, flour and parsley, fish cakes. We caught them by the dozens, gave them away by the dozens and made fish cakes by the dozens. Garfish was certainly not to be found in fish shops of which there were very limited numbers. I remember the fish man coming around on Friday nights to serve the Catholic needs.

He was usually a local fisherman. There was the odd place where fish and chips could be bought, but it often required going by bike or car. Since 2000 I have seen garfish in my local fish market and on menus and have even bought some to try to replicate the fish cakes. Somehow they did not taste the same.

On the way to school we were wont to drop a crab pot into the creek and collect the spoils on the way home. Catches included mud crabs, sand crabs and, on occasions, a few prawns. There is not and never will be anything quite like the mud crab, fresh from the water, boiled in the copper for dinner. In fact all seafood is different when eaten fresh from the water and with lemon and butter only. No fancy sauces! Sand whiting is one fish for which I have retained a passion. My younger brother David and I would head out across the mud flats to the mouth of the creek to fish the incoming tide for whiting and anything else that took the hook. On a late afternoon low tide it was, in retrospect, rather idyllic. On one occasion we were terrified to find ourselves, knee deep in water, with a small shark nosing around. I do wonder sometimes how we ever survived the freedom with which we were able to live and do things. Our father was the only one who was allowed to use the sharp knives so, if he was not around to fillet, we learned to cook them whole and eat them with lemon and butter.

And then there was the chook yard where there were chooks, bantams and ducks; and there were doves and pigeons. Bantams were treated as pets but chooks and ducks were for eggs and eating. Duck eggs make the most wonderful custard and Madeira cake. Afternoon tea was a fairly common part of life. Visitors came and out came the special afternoon tea table cloths, which my mother had hand embroidered in years past, the best china and the contents of the cake and biscuit tins. So we all kept up and extended our cake and biscuit making skills. This is when I learned to make biscuits in bulk, something which, when married myself, became a regular part of my life. With four children food seemed always to be in rather large quantities. Recipes were nowhere near as complicated and extravagant as they were later to become. Anzac biscuits, rock cakes, Weetbix slice and copha biscuits covered in hundreds and thousands were about the repertoire. Without anything as flash as an electric mixer we became very good at cooking sponge cakes. My eldest brother and I both entered our sponge cakes in the local Easter Show one year and, when his won, I lost interest in the sponge. This is also when I learned to cope with plucking and gutting poultry. Feathers were cleaned and kept for the feather eiderdown. I still bear a rather long, thin scar down the back of one thigh from when, as a very small child, I tried to rescue the duck whose head was about to drop from the chopping block. Doves or pigeons were another thing altogether. Catching them was quite an art. It required a cardboard box, a stick to prop one side up, a long piece of string and a few grains of chook feed or bits of bread. It needed a young person to crawl under the house out of sight and wait for the bird to start eating the seed placed under the box and then to pull the string and catch the bird. I did not mind the catching, plucking or stuffing parts, but I did object to the part that required wringing the neck. In my later years I came to know it on menus as squab.

Because of the many rather exotic fruits and vegetables grown in the home garden and by neighbours and friends we probably ate a far wider range of foods than most people and many things we grew and cooked have become part of modern menus: stuffed capsicums, stuffed marrow, snake beans, tamarillos. The acquisition of an electric frying pan started a passion for "rice a riso" or what we now know as risotto. Because it was a small seaside town in the 1940s and 1950s and because fried food was not something cooked in our house (or I suspect many homes of the day) potato chips were a treat to be waited for at the annual show. One bought iceblocks from the corner store. These were hand wrapped in paper and cost a penny each. The advent of the Silent Night refrigerator meant a limited number of iceblocks could be made at home and even ice cream, made with real cream, which I must say, never lasted long.

Boy Scouts and Girl Guides were another outlook for cooking skills. Canteen nights provided an opportunity to make the likes of fudge and peanut brittle, not part of the normal diet. Cooking over the outdoor fire was another associated treat, often practised in the back yard. I have no recollection at all of the barbecue as a cooking aid during these years. I do have though a wonderful memory of trying for my fire lighting badge in Girl Guides. We had tramped out to Finucane Creek on Finucane Road (this is now a major arterial road), collected our own firewood and set up our individual fires. Someone called out across the site: "You can only have two matches". This I heard as: "You can put some fat on it". My fire lit up beautifully on the first match well before anyone else's and I got my badge. One of the treats of camping was a peeled apple coated with brown sugar which caramelised in the flames and which could, with repeated dippings, be made to last for ages.

Entertaining and being entertained

I recall the first party for which I helped to plan and cook. My youngest brother, Harry, was turning eight and he had been promised a party! He and his young friends were mad keen on anything to do with cowboys and Indians. The traymobile was decked out as a covered wagon and taken into the garden, laden with hot dogs and corn on the cob. They were even permitted small bottles of Coke. We were accustomed to homemade cordial for which I cannot now find a recipe, but do recall both pineapple and lemon. The pineapple was made, I think, by stewing the skins. Imagine doing that today and imagine with what it might have been sprayed.

And so we lived on until, with a year in boarding school in Brisbane and four years living in college, I became somewhat disassociated from food and cooking. When in my early 20s, and when both parents were no longer alive, I first flatted on my own or with my youngest brother. I returned to the delights of planning and cooking meals, which has stayed with me ever since. In fact, I still start my day wondering what there might be for dinner. I remember travelling to work on the Manly Ferry in the 1970s with my husband and asking, "What would you like for dinner tonight", to be rebuffed with, "Why are you asking me that NOW???". This kind of thought preparation is not I suspect in the male psychological makeup!

In retrospect the gastronomic experience in Brisbane in the 1960s was pretty limited. Consequently my first experience of food that was really different happened on my first overseas excursion. In late December 1967, I went on a trip to Malaysia to stay with a Somerville House boarding school friend, Sue (Tan Suan Cheng) and her family. We had corresponded regularly since leaving school. Within an hour of my late night landing in Kuala Lumpur I had started putting on weight: first up was fried chicken at Petaling Jaya a sort of satellite suburb of Kuala Lumpur. On the following morning I was offered a breakfast of sweet cold coffee with raw egg! This is not something I could come at eating any time, much less first thing in the morning. We lunched at the Townhouse Hotel (Southern Cantonese style) with lots of little dishes. Finally home to the first home-cooked Chinese food, by which stage I was really beginning to love Chinese food. Eating mostly involved going out and trying different foods five to seven times a day: noodles for lunch, market shopping, beautiful fresh food dripping with water, tea English style around 4 pm, fresh lime drinks, to which I became addicted, pheasant and pheasant eggs with mushrooms and watercress. Later there was a home-cooked Christmas dinner of turkey, duck, chicken, crab, prawns, and coleslaw washed down with Nuit St Georges 1958. We then drove to the Cameron Highlands through dense forest to what looked like an English village with houses in the Tudor style. Afternoon tea was freshly picked strawberries with cream. Dinner was — Steamboat — a charcoal burner with the bubbling stock in the middle of the table and surrounded with finely cut and marinated pork, beef, abalone, prawns and vegetables. These were dropped into the bubbling broth and then fished out in a small net and eaten with relish. Whole fresh eggs were then broken into the by now rich stock, swirled around and the stock then drunk. I so thoroughly enjoyed this experience that I came home with a Steamboat and all of the equipment that went with it such as the little baskets. This, some 40 plus years later, I still have and still use. It is a bit like a fondue but far more exciting and inventive. Another memorable occasion was dinner at the Selangor Club in Kuala Lumpur. Here we had seafood cocktail, Dutch Aberdeen Angus beef steak and Australian lettuce salad, cheese and biscuits followed by Irish whiskey and cigars. It was certainly very cosmopolitan and very non-Oriental. This was followed by an invitation to a Punjabi dinner at the home of a medical practitioner. The invitation invited me to come early to see how it was prepared and cooked. It certainly was a very interesting experience watching chapatti cooked on a hot plate on an ordinary electric stove. The table was set with a pile of plates, the largest on the bottom and on top a rice pudding with raisins, AND, of all things, real silver spread on top. The chapatti was used as an eating implement as we worked our way down through the plates. Every now and then we got up to wash our hands at a hand basin in the corner of the room. It was certainly a very different meal and a very different way of doing things. And so it went on for something like three weeks. On my return to Brisbane I was interviewed by somebody on the ABC in relation to the gastronomic experience which I had had on my holidays.

I think probably one of the most interesting things that I learned on this expedition was that one did not have to be terribly ladylike with chopsticks. My Chinese hosts brought the bowl to the chin and quite literally shovelled the food in. This works remarkably well and I have continued to do it as often as practicable.

I am grateful to my mother for keeping the letters I wrote to her regaling all the delights of my first trip overseas.

Dinner parties and dining out

Without parents and with a career, the culinary life began to revolve around some restaurant eating, formal dinners in hotels and clubs and dinner parties. Italian food was a restaurant treat, provided in Brisbane by Mumma Luigi and the Milano: the Old Vienna did traditional European food; the Shingle Inn provided morning and afternoon tea treats.

I attribute the flush of home dinner parties in the 1960s and 1970s to population size and the dearth of enticing restaurants. Dining at home proved to be a viable and actually quite enjoyable alternative. Dinner parties were, on 20th century standards, exceedingly formal and formalised. Written invitations and acceptances were made: dress code was formal to the point where long frocks were worn by women: the best china and linen was used: menus were far less complex and daring.

When I had married and was living in Sydney in the early 1970s, I started to keep a "Dinner Diary". I employed a small five year diary with a name and address section to link people to dates. It served well as a memory of who had been offered what and when and thus avoided the embarrassment of always serving the same thing. By this time the formalities had become less observed and it was acceptable to invite by phone, while a thank you note was, however, still expected. The number of guests and no doubt the standard of cooking varied depending on whether planned or spontaneous. My husband would often ring my chambers leaving a message that he had invited some interstate or overseas visitor, with or without wife, to dinner "tonight". I would spend the ferry ride home working out a menu and a table setting, often grabbing some fish on the way from the shop on Manly Wharf.

These are some of the notes from the Dinner Diary, all of which I would have cooked myself:

> 4 Feb 1973 : Corned beef and fried cabbage; spiced raisin cake with custard
>
> 5 Feb 1973: Curried prawn quiche, stuffed herbed veal with potato bake and salads: mango mousse and chocolate torte.
>
> 11 June 1976: Prawn soup, rack of lamb, boiled potatoes and asparagus; hot fruit compote over ice cream.
>
> 14 July 1979: Pumpkin leek soup, fish roll and salad: banana coffee mousse, cheese and chocolates.
>
> 29 Oct 1982: Snapper chowder, ham and ratatouille, gooseberry and cream cheese mousse.

15 March 2015: Rockmelon soup, Prawn "risotto" made with quinoa, mandarin cake with cream.

Has anything changed very much over the years? The theory seems to be the same though the ingredients have moved on. I do wonder why it never occurred to me to order takeaway. I could count on one hand the number of times takeaway was ordered. In thinking about it they were occasions when there was no other alternative.

Formal functions like Bar Association annual dinners and celebratory events seemed to follow the same makeup and were not generally speaking memorable for the food. All fairly traditional!

At times there were unusually memorable occasions for cooking. In the early days of practising at the Bar in Brisbane, I was once chosen to produce a damper for morning tea for a visiting English Law Lord who had expressed a desire to go on a bushwalk. I had never made a damper and am sure it was not very good.

Volunteer cook

Lachlan had spent many of his school holidays going to camps of various kinds and when the school asked if anyone knew someone who could cook for a Crusader Union bike camp for 110 twelve year olds, Lachlan, without hesitation, nominated me. It was too difficult to refuse, but where to start. Thank goodness for the Church of England, who had obviously done this so often that they had produced a very instructive booklet on how to do it containing recipes, planning charts for meals, ingredients, quantities, shopping lists and examples. Oh for the advent of computers where an electronic spreadsheet would have made the task much easier and quicker. So out I went to Galston Gorge and a decent kitchen for seven days. It was up at 5 am for a cooked breakfast, production line for 110 plus sandwich lunches, then a morning of washing-up, making cakes, shopping and getting the dinner ready. Thank goodness that 12 year old boys were not then very fussy about food as long as there was plenty of it. It was bed at about 11 pm and then another exhausting day of the same. It was also my first introduction to gluten free food required for a celiac, which would later become my diet. The boy's mother had very wisely provided bread, various ingredients that might be useful and instructions. It was then easy to separate out cooking utensils and keep them isolated. We all survived if somewhat exhausted at the end of the week. It was not too long before I was asked to do a study week for a mixed group of Year 12s. This was quite a different exercise and experience. Seventeen year olds were fussy, picky, and in need of supper as well as all other meals. The planning worked the same and there was more housework. Enough! I decided that my holiday time could be spent with more emphasis on me. However, what I learned about planning ahead was a godsend.

Family cooking

Marriage and an acquired family meant more cooking and more food and more occasions around eating. With three stepsons keen to actually learn how to cook, progress was made. There was a house rule that if you wanted to go out after dinner and not be available for washing-up, there being no dishwasher then, you could cook instead. How good it was to have someone else thinking about dinner and producing it. There were meals for birthdays, family, visitors and celebrations of all kinds. No 1 Stepson (Archer) asked for a full roast dinner for his 21st. No 2 (Llew) craved an oriental night which, for 50 odd, became a complicated event with Chicken Chop Suey, Veal Curry and Fish Stew. No 3 (Lachlan) wanted all his favourite dishes for a lunch for 50 odd. By the time it came to James, he was into curries and could make most of them himself. Fortunately I had early experience of catering for large numbers and how to plan the food and organise the production thereof.

Twenty odd years of schoolboy sport meant that Saturday mornings could be hectic to the extreme. Without any intention for it to become so, Saturday became the day for soup and sandwiches and a family tradition. Huge pots of soup were made prior to the day including pea and ham, minestrone, chicken noodle, lamb and barley, and vegetable. Lunch was either in or out depending upon the location of the sporting event. The acquisition of a picnic basket and a very large thermos flask meant that it was possible to take enough food for at least four people to any sporting event. If it was possible to be at home, the expectation was that there would still be soup and sandwiches. As the years progressed, soup and sandwiches became a tradition in the B-W family for all sorts of occasions other than sporting events. When sporting days were over, soup, sandwiches and sherry for lunch on the Saturday became a familial event. When my husband retired from the workforce in 1983, his expectation was that there would be SOUP available on any day of the week for lunch. We used to joke about the old adage — I married you for life but not for lunch — by turning it into— I married you for life but not for soup for lunch in retirement. When my husband was dying and had decided that he would like to say farewell to his friends who were not aware of the coming event, the invitations went out for soup, sandwiches, sherry and salaams. Those invited knew at least what to expect in the food line.

With the advent of James and a growing family with daughters-in-law and grandchildren, planning for family gatherings became more critical. Having decided it was time to share the load, I took to setting the menu and then inviting contributions. This was generally maintained in the planning of most extended family gatherings, including the launch of the B-W family history book attended by just over 100 people, birthdays, Christmases, farewells and visitors.

Memorable meals

Along the way there were some meals, memorable not only for the food but for the occasion. The first Steamboat in the Cameron Highlands in Malaysia became a very familiar part of family life. The basic soup and sandwiches occasions which were so comforting and so easy were so heart-warming in many ways. The first meal in a New York Diner — scrod - with what seemed like an infinite choice of accompanying potatoes and salad dressings was an interesting experience. Scrod for those who like me had no idea what scrod is, was a large-fleshed white fish something like cod. And then there was a private dinner at L'Ambroisie, a restaurant in the Place des Vosges, Paris in celebration of the 40th birthdays of my goddaughter and her husband noted in **Things Peripatetic**. It was an evening to remember. There were about 10 to 12 small degustation dishes and the most exquisite wines to go with them.

Cooking for one

Living alone as I have done for over 20 years now has not altered my enthusiasm for food or home-cooked food. I do not mind cooking for one and eating alone. My meals, like my reading, are an eclectic mix of old and new recipes and cooking methods. The gift of a tagine introduced a different cooking style and an excuse to invite neighbours into share. Slow cooking is very much in vogue as I write and my original Crock-Pot in colours of orange and brown has come out of the cupboard again. If there is food left over, or no guests to share, it gets portioned and frozen for later. Over 20 years ago the elders in the family started to host, in rotation, a breakfast on the Sunday before Christmas. It continues with some of the elders replaced by those of the next generation. Each host delights in providing something different each year.

In recent years my cousin, Eve Abbey, and I have taken to weekend meals where we each provide one course agreed upon for all sorts of reasons — the purchase of a lovely little lamb roast or prawns or just a craving for roast vegetables. Many of the recipes for sweets come out of a shared familial past — lemon sago, mango sago, rice pudding, lemon delicious to name but a few.

So eating is a great occupation whatever the current culinary fads might be, but whetting the appetite is enhanced by the ever-growing choice of beautiful fresh food in this country.

A good culinary experience would seem to need a place, company, food and conversation. Whereas that was once a home with special friends or family, eating home-cooked food and enjoying spirited conversation on many topics, today it is more likely to be a restaurant, club, pub or footpath café, with a friend or relative, a business associate or work colleague or even the person you were inviting to dinner who insists on "going to a restaurant". There will be a choice of Thai, Italian, Moorish, Spanish, Indian, Greek, French … cuisine. There will inevitably be a mobile phone or tablet within reach and deafening noise making interesting conversation virtually impossible.

Each to his own. I still relish the morning foray into the cupboards and the refrigerator to make a decision about what I will eat tonight, how I will cook it and possibly with whom I shall share it.

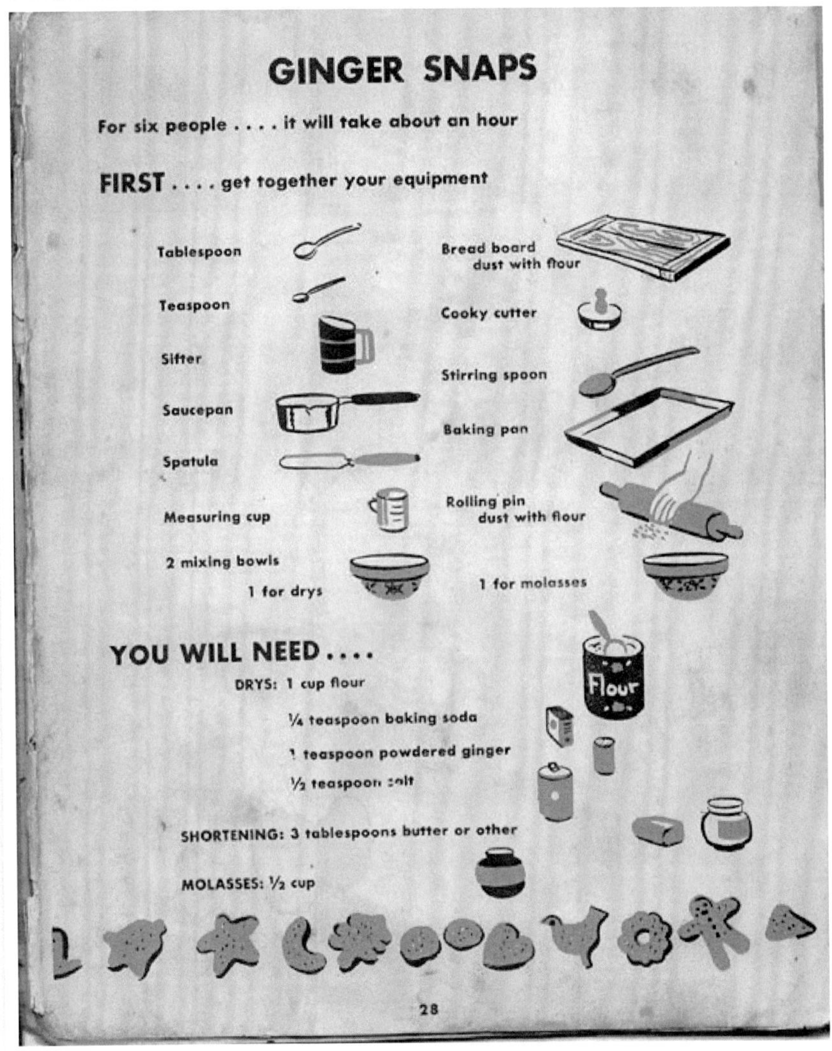

GINGER SNAPS

For six people . . . . it will take about an hour

FIRST . . . . get together your equipment

YOU WILL NEED . . . .

DRYS: 1 cup flour

¼ teaspoon baking soda

1 teaspoon powdered ginger

½ teaspoon salt

SHORTENING: 3 tablespoons butter or other

MOLASSES: ½ cup

28

First recipe book.

8. Things Domestic

Things Domestic — Habitation — Relocating— Housekeeping — Sewing — Renovating — Decorating — Lifestyles

Charles Lamb to Thomas Hood on leaving Colebrooke Cottage on 18 September 1827:

> "To change habitations is to die to them, and in my time I have died seven deaths. But I don't know whether every such change does not bring with it a rejuvenescence. Tis an enterprise, and in the sense of death's approximating, which tho' not terrible to me, is at all times particularly distasteful."

Lucas, E V, *The Life of Charles Lamb,* Vol II, at 723 (Methuen, 1905).

Habitations

If Charles Lamb be right I have died 17 deaths and happily survived all the rejuvenating experiences.

When the Second World War broke out we were living at Cleveland and it was here that my father enrolled in the Australian Army as a sergeant cook along with two of my mother's brothers. He was attached to the units moving up the Queensland coast towards Townsville. He was a severe asthmatic and the further north he travelled the more difficult and pronounced his medical condition became and he was discharged early in the activities. Finding employment at that time was difficult and in consequence we moved around to wherever suitable work was available in South East Queensland. By the time we returned to live in Cleveland in 1948 we had lived in seven different places. My memories are mainly of particular incidents rather than of the places themselves until I was a little older. It was at Coopers Plains that my younger brother, David, disappeared and a search party was sent out to look for him. He was eventually found sound asleep beneath the counter of the shop where the lolly tins were kept. It was also at Coopers Plains where my older brother, Jim, decided that I should hold the nail while he hammered it into a piece of timber. In consequence of this I have a split nail on my left hand which has remained in that state. It was here also that, chasing each other around the house, Jim dived under a bed, split his tongue on the edge of the bedpost and ended up with eight stitches in his tongue and having to live on jelly, ice cream and spaghetti. While all this was happening young David had gone to sleep in the bath while the nanny was preoccupied. At Roma, we decided to emulate our father's barbering skills and to cut each other's hair using an upturned highchair as the barber's chair. It was rather cold out at Roma and we spent quite a bit of time wearing pixie hoods to disguise the very poor hairstyles we had created. Esk was where Jim started school: he remembers walking to school in Esk over what seemed a "massive bridge" which he now thinks must have shrunk more than a little. Ballandean was where I started school. Ballandean was also where I took a candle with me to bed and, putting it beside the bed on the floor, the bedspread caught fire. I think Stanthorpe was the first place in which we lived with electricity but it still had a wooden stove and an outdoor toilet. How life has changed.

In Auckland in New Zealand we stayed for several months with Aunt Edna Holden and daughter Evelyn. My memories of Auckland are few but revolve around rain, rain and more rain, cousin Eve's glass eye in the bathroom, Aunt Edna's fabulous collection of haberdashery and going to a movie about someone losing an eye and me sitting on the floor facing backwards for the duration. Brothers Jim and David missed out on a ride on an elephant when the queue closed just as it was their turn. David subsequently blames everything that goes wrong in his life on missing out on that ride on the elephant at the Auckland Zoo.

Cleveland was where my multi-skilled father built the house that was my home until I was 23. It was, I believe from family anecdotes, built out of recycled cedar packing cases that had housed aircraft parts. He also built a wooden rotating clothes line which served very well and survived the passage of time. As children we turned into fairly willing helpers and were provided with carpenter's aprons and taught how to use hammers and hand drills. When it came time to build some gardens we learnt to hoe and shovel, compost, rake and mow with a hand lawn mower, water with water from the well and to trim and weed. There was a fresh water well which pumped to a small tank under which there was a shower which was a godsend when coming back from the beach covered in salt and sand. We had ducks and chooks which needed feeding with feeding troughs that needed cleaning. We had birds in cages that needing looking after. We were also adept at catching pigeons using a string attached to a box with grain underneath, the catch from which Daddy would stuff with goodies. Today it is called squab and is a luxury item on menus around the world. We grew radishes, parsley, strawberries and sweet peas for market and were inducted as helpers. It was a place where we were always very busy. It was also a place where there was neither town water nor a sewerage system and remained that way until we left Cleveland in 1965. It was also the place where I acquired most of my domestic skills: gardening, sewing, knitting, washing, washing-up, ironing, cooking, house cleaning and floor polishing using polishing wax. Cleveland was also the place where I acquired many of what might be called my athletic skills: swimming, bike riding, running, tennis, cricket, vigoro and basketball. My attempt at long jump off the low verandah, while my mother talked to the local GP, was not very successful though as I ended up with a starred ankle and plaster cast above my knee for three months. It was a very good place in which to grow up. And grow up we did when my mother went back to teaching and, as married women returning to the work force were not permitted to teach where their children went to school, we became latch-key children with many little responsibilities. We collected the meat for dinner from the butcher, checked the crab pot on the way home from school, picked and prepared the vegetables, brought in the washing, attended to the watering of the garden and whatever else might have needed to be done. It was very good training for later on. Domesticity was not to be shunned: it was challenging and enjoyable and a great learning experience.

My father died unexpectedly in 1957. I left Cleveland in 1965 with my mother and youngest brother, Harry, to rent at Toowong in Brisbane where we stayed until my mother died in 1968. Harry and I then flatted in Toowong. The first home that I owned was a unit on Coronation Drive, Toowong, in Brisbane: second on the left from the City was the direction I used to give visitors. It was in a brand new strata title building with six only units and was not fully occupied. With only a basic kitchen and bathroom, it was decorator's heaven — or so I thought. With the help of an experienced friend I chose white walls, dark carpet and in-vogue orange kitchen cupboards and set about making curtains in a variety of fabrics. It was a bit like playing cubbies as a child — all that freedom to do as one chose. It was virtually on the finishing line for the Head of the River and a good place for entertaining. It brought me my first experience of running a Strata Title Scheme. It taught me never to even contemplate buying another penthouse unit with a flat roof above, though one saving grace might have been that the 1973 flood did not make it to the third floor.

When I married and moved to Sydney in 1971, David had recently acquired a late Victorian detached dwelling with a later rooftop addition, accessed by a spiral staircase, at Fairlight, near Manly. It was conveniently located not far from Manly Wharf and the Fairlight harbour pool, with both of which we became very familiar: it was spacious and roomy enough for the stepsons to bring home their friends on exeat weekends: it was surrounded by friendly neighbours: it was, however, in need of some TLC which was slowly tackled. The spiral staircase was demolished and a proper wooden staircase installed and an ensuite bedroom built in to the upper floor. A workshop and later a cubbyhouse were built in the back yard: drainage was attacked with gusto and I laboured over miles of curtain material. We worked hard on making it a comfortable home and enjoyed living there. We entertained, had many visitors to stay and spent hours on the local beaches. It was with much regret that we decided to move after the residents of a small block of four flats next-door turned into the neighbours from hell and one of them tried to strangle David with his own tie for responding to a cry for help from a young woman. The Manly police could not have been more co-operative and helpful, but we could not bear the thought of more of the same.

We moved to a huge block at North Balgowlah with an above ground swimming pool and room for a half-size cricket pitch which did not take long in coming. It was in a very quiet cul de sac and no units in site. It had been built by a builder as his own home and needed very little work. There were more curtains to make, however, and a decent-sized garden with which to play. It meant a herb and vegetable garden and a compost heap and, with a number of existing fruit trees, plenty of fruit for jam and marmalade. James became a weekly boarder at Shore Prep in 1983 and this freed me up to spend more days in Chambers each week. There was a bus at the corner which took me to the city in good time. The commodious house was two storeyed and, downstairs, half of it was devoted to a large rumpus room with a sandstone rock face at one end. In went a table tennis table and a pot belly stove. It was the perfect place for entertaining adults, children and teenagers, for partying and vegging out. The pot belly not only kept the house warm but served as the winter stove. The ping-pong table served additionally as somewhere to cut out materials for sewing. There was space and a place to leave my sewing machine ready at all times to do mending or to sew without having to put it away in a cupboard when not in use. We ate downstairs most of the winter months. We Christmased down there, we held post-wedding receptions, birthday parties, family reunions, a farewell dinner for James and friends when he and classmate Tim set off to France on an student exchange. We once accommodated most of an Indian schoolboy cricket team down there. We launched the Boddam-Whetham family history book in the garden in 1987 with over a hundred people in attendance.

There was a study/office/spare bedroom downstairs with an external entrance which became David's retreat when he retired from the Public Service. He found a neighbour who was willing to type and set about being a consultant for the Pipeline Authority, the Electricity Commission and various local authorities around NSW. There was a TAFE College within walking distance at Seaforth and David enrolled in HSC mathematics in order to keep up with James. The suburb may not have been the most popular in Sydney but was one in which it was easy to live comfortably and happily. It was close to beaches and walking tracks which occupied much of our time. We could ride our bikes to the beach. What more could anyone ask?

The neighbourhood was friendly and co-operative and the cat knew exactly which neighbour's house to go to for food when we were away. When our aged neighbour could no longer manage his large yard we found ourselves doing the odd chore. Another neighbour, who was French, willingly invited James into her home for French conversation while she was preparing dinner at night. We all lived side by side in harmony with no aggravation. It was easy to take. It was also 13 years and 1990 before we realised that James was heading to University with College life and would be far less inclined to cross not only the Harbour Bridge but also the Spit Bridge as well to come home. It was then that we started to think about a future without a huge house and garden. So we set about making separate lists of what we needed or would like and what we did not want. David needed a swimming pool, a library, the smallest amount of garden and house maintenance, something that could be safely left to go travelling and not far from the city. He had followed up an invitation from the Sydney Grammar School Old Boys Union to put the past in touch with the present and had started to give time to working with the Sydney Grammar School Foundation towards this end. This was an occupation which he was even reluctant to give up shortly before he died. He had no wish to retire into the country as some of his friends had done. I listed my needs for a library close by, public transport to the city, a small garden if possible and not too much housework. I was certainly not ready to move into the country. We set about making the Balgowlah home ready to sell and spent a good 18 months researching various localities that might satisfy our stated requirements. We homed in on certain streets in Cremorne and around North Sydney. When we found an un-abused terrace in North Sydney (not far from Shore School after nine years going to and from for various activities!) being privately sold and which required some work, but not too much, we actually bought the terrace before we had finalised the sale of Balgowlah North. With a paint job and a new carpet we were able to move in. Drainage was an issue as, in many of the old terraces in Sydney, rainwater water from the roof drained into the ground beneath the downpipe. David was what you might describe as being obsessed with rising damp and proper drainage. It was to be the third house he had drained properly in Sydney. The backyard was dug up, drainage was extended from the rear of the house out to the front street and a drainage pit with a pump, which came on automatically when water was at a certain height, was installed. We familiarised ourselves with the locality, walking the local streets at all hours of the day and night, locating various facilities and interesting places. We became addicted to the early morning walk around Ball's Head.

There were a couple of spare bedrooms; family friends, nephews, nieces and visitors were welcome. There were French exchange students who played scrabble in English, borrowed camping gear and left their ski boots in a cupboard for when "I come back". There was a sleepover for ex-boarders from Somerville House when one from far north Queensland visited Sydney; the grandchildren came for their birthday sleepovers and treats; Christmases and birthdays were celebrated in the courtyard garden. Life was no less busy but we adapted to the challenges of a different lifestyle with enthusiasm and relish. When David was diagnosed with terminal pancreatic cancer in November 1993, James' French exchange hosts were in town. So as not to spoil their visit they were told he had gallstones. With a time line of 2 weeks to 10 months and advice to do whatever could be done with reasonable comfort we put all else aside and did whatever was fancied: picking blackberries and making jam, hopefully like his mother made at Balmoral Beach, a glamorous weekend in the Blue Mountains, a trip to Canberra to see an old friend and on to Thredbo for the start of the fourth leg of the Federation Track to Melbourne. I left him there with his walking friends who had no idea he was ill. He made it to the end of the leg at Mt Hotham but came home a little weary. We sorted necessary paper work. He visited the crematorium to ensure his place under the family tree, and when he asked if there would be enough money for a wake, I suggested an open house. Very few people knew of his illness. When invited to an At Home "sustained by sherry, soup and sandwiches and by your salutations, salaams and salvos", most turned up thinking it was his birthday. It was obvious that he was very, very ill. What a way to bow out.

I stayed on: James came home for his honours' year. I rented a beach house at Patonga to get away from the dramas of weekends of thesis writing. James won an Australia Federation of Advertising Award and joined Singletons for a year's training, worked on Labor Party Accounts and the Republican Yes Campaign. James went overseas, came back and started with university friends, Yap, a website for tertiary students. I was so fully absorbed with law reporting and converting the reports to digital that I did not notice the passing of time. It took a while to wonder what I was doing virtually alone in a four bedroom terrace with 34 stairs to the top. I decided a unit without any maintenance somewhere in the locality which I had come to know and love was the answer. I managed to sell before I bought, rented a flat and set about seriously looking for something suitable. That something turned up faster than anticipated at McMahons Point not far from the ferry wharf but in need of complete refurbishment. For once I did not have to live through it and allowed the experts to make the major decisions. It was just as well that I had a temporary roof over my head. I moved in in September 1999 and have not regretted the move for a moment. A view of the Harbour to die for was not on my wish list and is an endless source of interest, entertainment and delight. Needless to say I sometimes forget it is there. I frequently ignore fireworks displays. There are so many of them. James stayed in the flat I had rented as an interim measure, came here for a short time and started life on his own sharing with friends.

At the end of the day you make a life and a lifestyle out of what you have, not what others may have, nor what you are missing or think you are missing.

The house my father built at Cleveland. This is also the only photograph of the whole family. It was taken by Sue Tan on an exeat weekend from Somerville House.

House at North Balgowlah.

The rumpus room at north Balgowlah which had so many uses.

Cricket pitch. Pool and hammock. What more could one want?

The view from McMahons Point late one day when the setting sun was reflected from the clouds in the East.

9. Things Sportive

Things Sportive — Participation — Juvenile — Teenage — Adult — Parent — Spectator — Bushwalker

While it is now universally accepted that it is good for man to be fit and healthy it was not always so. The ascendancy of sport today is remarkable not only for participation and media coverage but for extreme varieties. The more extreme the more popular it seems to become. Gym attendance seems to be compulsory at whatever stage of life one is in. Running and cycling and walking are all very popular sports of the day. Some of the sports today could not be less likely to make man fit and healthy, particularly for his life after the particular sport. The ageing process brings to our attention all those little bits and pieces that might be in better condition had we not undertaken such exciting and arduous pastimes.

Juvenile years

My very first recollection of anything that might be vaguely described as athletic or sporting was at about the age of five going to a dam outside Stanthorpe with the family. None of us could swim that I recall but my father put me into a rubber tyre pushed me around the pool and left me to float as though I was on a boat. Unfortunately I wriggled around enough to upturn the tyre and went down into water over my head. I can still see the dark and the stars which terrified me before somebody pulled me out. Something of that incident stayed with me because I never became a confident swimmer even though I spent a lot of my time when young swimming at the beach or in pools.

When we lived in Cleveland there were numerous places we could swim either from the beach or off a jetty in a constructed pool. I don't recall ever having a formal swimming lesson and it was not until I went to secondary school that I actually learned to swim and breathe correctly. The beaches at Cleveland were not surfing beaches and I never learned to surf though I did go to surfing beaches from time to time.

At primary school we did athletics including a lot of handball sports. I was quite a fast little runner and was even chosen to represent the district in the State Athletics Carnival. We played basketball and vigoro as team sports. Vigoro is a game not well known today but it was very similar in many ways to cricket. Differences included rules about running if you hit halfway down the crease thus making it a very fast game and being able to pitch rather than bowl overarm. I became quite a good bowler by pointing my left finger down the pitch and pitching towards that point. We played both basketball and vigoro in competition with other local schools. We played tennis and this was one sport where we did have some coaching from a local parent. There was a family tradition that one got a tennis racquet for one's 10th birthday. As my older brother was a year ahead of me he had a tennis racquet and I did not. He was always looking for somebody to play with him at home. Consequently I became reasonably competent playing tennis with a light cricket bat until my 10th birthday.

We probably spent more time riding our bikes than anything else in our early years. We rode to and from school, we rode to the shops, we rode to the beach or to the swimming pool at the end of the jetty, my cousin and I rode to the cemetery to look after our grandparents' grave, we went on discovery excursions at the weekend where we tossed a coin at the corner — heads we go left, tails we go right — and ended up in places where I am sure our parents may not have wished us to be. We were taught to fix our bikes ourselves, to change our tyre tubes and chains and not to leave the bikes lying about. AND we did not have mobile phones or GPS but always managed to get home in time for dinner.

Teenage years

As I headed off to secondary school at the age of 14 — there being only four years of high school before matriculation — the only activity which I continued seriously was athletics. I represented my house in inter-house competitions and the school in the inter-school competitions. I did, however, continue to play tennis at home at the weekends and to play some competition tennis in the Redlands area. The bike was still there to be used for necessary activities that were not part of everyday living in the way that it had been before. I never played basketball or vigoro again. I was, however, introduced to a more serious form of cricket as a spectator when my brothers took me to the 1960 Test match against West Indies at the Brisbane Cricket Ground as a birthday present. That was the Test which was tied and we were sitting on the hill with a glorious view of all the activity. It was a very exciting day. In later years I was to spend a great deal of time on the sidelines at cricket matches.

University and beyond

Athletics stayed with me for a couple of years at university where I participated in inter-college athletics carnivals. There were many inter-college and inter-faculty sporting activities and it was here that I was inducted into a serious role as a spectator. The Law Faculty was very small in numbers and those participating in inter-faculty sporting activities were keen to have supporters on the side lines. It was Leo Williams who tried to teach me the rules of rugby so that I would know what I was looking at. He even took me to a major game at Lang Park where I recall little of the game but do recall a coloured smoke bomb going off. Tennis was not so easy to play and I took up squash with a few friends who played. It did not require a lot of planning and could be played at night as well as during the day. This was also about the time that tenpin bowling became popular and it was a pleasant activity to undertake with a few friends from time to time.

After three years at university as a full-time student I became a part-time student because of my commitment to articles of clerkship as a law student. They were long, full days with very little time for commitment to any kind of regular sporting activity. I played a bit of squash and became a regular spectator at inter-faculty activities. Once I entered into full-time employment there was little time for regular sporting activities at all and I found myself becoming a bushwalker when I took time out for relaxation at places like Binna Burra on the Lamington Plateau and at Mermaid Beach on the Gold Coast with my friend Jean Russell. I have continued to enjoy walking to the present day.

Sydney

When I came to live in Sydney it was to Fairlight near Manly. At the bottom of the street there was a swimming pool in the Harbour. This suited me perfectly because it was not surf. I was quite content to swim there as often as possible and leave my husband and his sons to go to the surfing beaches not far away. When James was born there was a period when I worked from home. Every day I pushed a pram down to that little beach with its pool for an hour or so of playing in the sand and swimming in the pool. In consequence James became quite a good swimmer. I played squash with the teenagers and took part in the odd game of tenpin bowls. I even played comp tennis with a group of local friends for a few years.

It was here though that I became a long-term spectator. David's three boys all participated for their schools in, variously, cricket, rugby, athletics and swimming. And so began 22 years of schoolboy sport from the side-lines. Sometimes the boys were at the same location, other times they were playing miles apart. It is to be recommended as a good exercise in learning one's way around a new city or town. It was not only schoolboy sport though as David had played both baseball and cricket in his youth and kept up interests in both games. James was still in a pram when David took up a challenge to captain a fifths team for the Manly Club. Grounds were as far apart as Sutherland and Hornsby. I think that I eventually got to know every cricket ground in Sydney. With membership of the Sydney Cricket Ground there were days devoted to following Sheffield Shield as well as Test games. We all spent many enjoyable days at the SCG with friends. When James entered primary school he took on swimming, cricket and soccer where he hankered for the position of goalie so he could do "athletic things". When he was forced to give up rugby at Shore because of loose joints he took to soccer and earned a GPS position as goalkeeper. He continued to play soccer until well into his thirties. I recall one occasion on which I umpired for an under-10 cricket team when no suitable father turned up. I frequently scored for the Shore Prep teams.

My connection with cricket is long and full of pleasant memories. At the Bar in Brisbane I became the official scorer for the barristers v solicitors annual game and once had a bat on the Gabba in one of those games. The first time I went out with David was to watch a cricket match at

Southport between the Wanderers and the I Zingari. Friends who knew nothing about cricket once asked us to take the Earl of Inchcape, who was visiting from UK, to the Hill for a day at the Sydney Cricket Ground. That was all he wanted to do, so out we went with best rug and the basket full of goodies. He thoroughly enjoyed himself and contacted us for years afterwards when he was out here. He never asked to go back to the Hill though thank goodness. When James made the firsts at Shore I became part of the mothers' afternoon tea brigade at Northbridge. My very favourite photo is one taken by the headmaster of James and his father at the annual game between fathers and sons at Northbridge with James wearing his father's hat and David wearing the Shore Firsts' cap.

Bushwalking

Of all the physical activities I have undertaken walking in the bush has got to be the most pleasurable. Wherever I have lived there has always been somewhere to go for a walk in the morning or the evening. When all else fails walking around the local neighbourhood can be full of pleasant surprises. When first working I discovered Binna Burra in the Lamington Mountains. I could not wait for any opportunity to go back and explore. I thrice walked/climbed Mt Warning with family members and friends. Sydney is so green with hidden pathways and myriads of beaches that there is a never-ending supply of places to discover and discovering is what I have done since arriving. David had always been a keen and intrepid walker so many weekends were spent going somewhere we had not been before and pottering around. When he became involved in overseeing the construction of a gas pipeline from Sydney to Newcastle he kept saying that he was going to walk that easement one day. That day came sooner than expected when the Inaugural Great North Walk (GNW) from Sydney to Newcastle was advertised in 1988. He could not wait to join in. It was a supported walk over three weeks undertaken by a mixed group of people who got on so well together that they decided to continue walking together after reaching Newcastle.

And so began the Wombat Walkers and years of regular planned weekend walks in and around Sydney, plus a two night camp somewhere each October and a Harbour picnic each January. The Wombats are still going but not quite as strongly as they began. As I was working full-time, I could not join the Great North Walk but joined the Wombats and for many years have kept the monthly newsletter going. We greet each other like long-lost friends at the beginning of every walk, move up and down the track catching up with everyone at some stage and enthusing on the landscape or the shape of trees as well as swapping news and ideas. Our leader, Leigh Shearer-Heriot aka Dr Wombat, is addicted, having been one of the planners and organisers of the Great North Walk. He has an uncanny knack of finding somewhere to walk where we have never been before.

Not only did the Great North Walk give birth to the Wombats but also to the Federation Track from Sydney to Melbourne. It was first undertaken by members of the Wombats and others in the early 1990s and led by Bill Avery. In his guide to the *Federation Track from Circular Quay to Stanwell Park,* Bill says: "during one of the Wombat Walks, David Boddam-Whetham raised the suggestion that a bushwalk from Sydney to Melbourne would be something of an adventure. I was immediately interested and excited at this idea, but purely as a retirement project … The Great North Walk 'lifers' became the backbone of the Federation Track Walkers over the following years". David was able to complete the first three legs of the Federation Track — in all some 1200kms. James and I walked into Melbourne at the end of the fourth leg with a bottle of port which David had ceremoniously handed over to James for the final dinner in Melbourne. In 1991 David wrote a piece for Bill's book titled *On walking in a Group:*

> "When walking together, there is far more communication than is experienced by people who are merely journeying. Talking is not the prime factor, as many of the group prefer silence and in some cases go to extreme lengths to be on their own — walking either way out in front of the group or trailing far behind. Discussions among walkers cover an enormous range of subjects. There are the topics you would expect: flowers, birds, phenomena of the bush, even geology. Feet, boots and equipment also feature as these are themes of discussion for all bushwalkers. However, in a good walking group, the conversation ranges widely over personal experiences, philosophies, personalities and a gradual sharing of views on life and values. Some people move about the group, constantly interacting, constantly improving relationships; others, although not sullen tend to walk alone and wait for talkers to come to them."

What a wonderful conceptualisation of the walking spirit.

Qi Gong

While I continue to walk wherever and whenever I can, I find it both calming and energising of body and mind to stop and to do Qi Gong. I have done a couple of day courses at WEA and have a very useful video for when I forget the sequences.

Things sportive include more of the things that provide nurture to the mind especially when chosen for the many pleasures they provide as diversions from the trials and tribulations of life.

Father and son at the Father and Son's Shore First's cricket match.

The Spirit of the Federation Track in contemplative mood as ever.

Out in the bush in 2011.

10. Things Mellow

Things Mellow — Memory — Medicalisation — Grandparenting — Decluttering — Azygous living

There comes a time in all of our lives hopefully when our characters and personalities are softened or matured by age or experience and we may be more relaxed, more easygoing, more placid and maybe more low maintenance. It is in this mellowed state that I undertook this task of putting together some memorabilia — some things whether remarkable or worthy to be recorded — of my life and times and to here identify some of the things which were relevant to living through a life of being and doing.

Memory

I seem to have spent a great deal of my life walking and talking to myself in my head. I composed documents, arguments, letters and such like in my head before putting pen to paper for most of my working life. I have also been an advocate of lists and outlines. I do, however, worry about memory — particularly mine — and what it seems to be doing to me. I am beginning to think that what I have done over the years is to train my memory into very bad habits. I seem to be rather good at putting things into a file somewhere — for later on. I suspect it is rather like using a computer, and putting things into hidden files. The major problem is that when I want to retrieve that little bit of memory I have great difficulty finding it. I have forgotten the password. Some of it may have had to do with learning the law. Because of the huge amount of the reading which we were required to do, it became necessary to learn the principles **and** where to find the detail if necessary. Still that is no excuse.

It may have something to do with not socialising with people. Because of the nature of the work that I did, I spent a great deal of time with a pencil in my hand and a piece of paper in front of me. Since my husband died I have not had anybody on tap to talk to in the same way that I was able to talk with him. In fact, he was absolutely amazing in the way that he could pick up on any topic upon which my fertile mind would want to labour. He was a chemical engineer and after running companies for Shell and Ampol for many years ran the Energy Department for the New South Wales Government. Now — I find myself writing a list of the things about which I want to talk to various people coming through my life. When my son came to have dinner with me on a Sunday evening, I would have a list of things about which to talk, which I would tick off before he left. When I meet a special friend for lunch, I go with a list of things I want to talk to her about just in case I forget something I really wish to raise with her. It seems a bit silly, but it does work. I sometimes think that I should go around the house talking out loud so that the thoughts in my head are actually memorised in a more retrievable way. I suspect the good old rote learning had a lot going for it.

It has made me wonder about the ways in which we were taught. I know that things have improved and changed remarkably and I would love to think that I could go back and learn a lot of those things again. This time though I would hope to be able to retain them more accessibly. But then of course that may not be the way of things. Word processing and the Internet have made everything retrievable, except it would seem individual memories. They may be good and useful aides-memoire but are not the real thing. I am amused by the meaning of "memory bank" in the *Macquarie Dictionary* as "the primary storage inside the main part of a computer to which fast random access is available". Oh for one of those in my head, especially with the fast random access.

It is also interesting when doing something like the current activity on ***Things Done*** to reflect on memory and how it works in this kind of exercise. Everybody has different memories of the same occasion. It is rather interesting to watch them told in totally different ways. I have three brothers and our memories of particular incidents in our childhood are so completely different on occasions that one wonders how that could possibly be. We were obviously different ages with different trained memories and with different insights into the world. I think that Steven Carroll may have found an answer in *Forever Young* (2015, Fourth Estate, at 292-293) where he suggests that the act of looking back "prompts the thought that we are never one life, but a succession of lives, never one self, but a succession".

Medicalisation

The further we get from our youthful stage the closer we seem to get to our medical advisers. Aging and maturing processes together with advances in medical science seem to be producing a mountain of ills and ailments never seen or contemplated before. If it is not eyes, it is hips and knees: if it is not memory it may be skin. Be rest assured that whatever it is or might be will need investigating. The simple question "How are you?" can bring a response of encyclopaedic proportions. How does one curb the response, which may just provide some information that is useful? How does one avoid the process and consequences? Being prone to extreme reactions to chemical smells and having once been taken from a newly renovated Opera House drama theatre to emergency, with blood pressure off the scale, I have become the subject of a quarterly maintenance check. It makes one think of putting the car in for regular maintenance. Needless to say both processes are reassuringly comforting in their own way. In company it is best to avoid the topic and, if that is not always possible, to suggest that medical topics, in the same way as politics and religion have been socially eschewed, be avoided.

Grandparenting

Is there a right time or age to become a grandparent? What does being a grandparent mean or involve? I never knew a grandparent on either side of the family tree and nor has my son. There were older people in our lives whom we called Aunty or Uncle but they were friends of our parents and nothing more. How does one react when it happens? When David's first grandchild arrived our son was still in primary school and his reaction was

"I am not ready to be a grandfather". It was not long, however, before he was happily befriending and entertaining a granddaughter and soon thereafter her brother. Until they reached 18 their birthday treat was a weekend spent with us doing whatever they chose. There was never any obligation to babysit or baby mind or take on any other regular commitment. Other grandchildren arrived but, unfortunately, were GI (Geographically Impossible) living too far away for us to become closely involved in their lives. One wonders if they suffered in any way. When they became young adults they also became distanced and eventually some have become parents with lives of their own and their own willing grandparents in tow. I had to wait until James was in his late 30s before he became a father. I was nearly 70 and like close friend Lesley wondered if it was too late to take up this role. Fortunately kinship seems to work osmotically. Without any commitment to regular minding, I took on the odd minding and the occasional emergency when the nanny did not turn up. Claude and then Auguste and I have become good friends. Since they went to California in 2014, we Skype, I send email stories, I visit, and Claude visits with Dadda for a fortnight and has a ball going to all the old familiar places with one or other of the local grandmothers. It is a very special relationship and long may it last.

Decluttering

Declutter is not a word I can find in any of my dictionaries. Go to the Internet though and there are literally thousands of references. There is help and advice on: decluttering and reorganising; how to fix clutter and relocate; 10 creative ways to declutter your home; nine decluttering secrets from professional organisers; decluttering any room in your home with these tips, techniques and ideas; eight game changing decluttering lessons; de-clutter safely and effectively and help avoid relapse; health benefits of decluttering; power decluttering; rules of decluttering. The family have left home, there are boxes of all sorts of things stored somewhere around the unit or garage: there are things closeted which might come in handy some day: there are family heirlooms as to which no one seems inclined to be responsible: there are duplicates of things such as china and cutlery that have been collected across the years: there are clothes that have not been worn for decades but are kept for sentimental reasons: there are books by the metre from which one cannot be parted: the years are adding on and what is going to happen to all of it and who is going to take responsibility and do something about it? The time has come for a mature approach to making those decisions that the next generation does not and will not want to make and to declutter. But where does one start?

I actually started years ago but it never seems to end. Every house move has involved getting rid of something that does not fit or is no longer needed. I then began to look each week for two things I no longer needed. It then became each day. Most of them go somewhere out of the house or out of sight to be rethought at a later time. Books are culled at least once a year and go to a worthy cause. Mending or altering clothes is viewed in a different light. Anything complicated means it goes out. There are 50 years of appointment diaries and duplicates of paperwork that can go after this exercise is complete. Many have not proved to be very useful. As advised, there are lists of paraphernalia being continually updated to go with my will. There are stickers and notes with provenances going on to the back of paintings and pieces of furniture. I try hard to give to family and friends things they may like but, perhaps fortunately for them, they are not acquisitively minded. I will persevere while wondering if anyone will heed the instructions or be receptive to the gift. Onward, ever onward!

Art and Literature

With time and patience on one's hands art and literature of all descriptions come again to the fore. There are so many books to read, so many plays and films to go to the choices are hard. Why waste time on something that is not enjoyable or to one's liking. Time is running out. Don't like what is on TV, switch it off. Not enjoying a film or a play, get up and leave. Not liking a book, toss it aside or take it back to the library.

Azygous living

When or where or why I came in contact with this wonderful word I have no recollection at all, but I do remember signing myself "Azygously yours" in a letter to my husband before we were married. It has stuck in the back of my mind ever since and been retrieved on various strange occasions. Its origins are embedded in the Greek language and it means "unwedded, not constituting one of a pair". In anatomy it means "pertaining or relating to anything occurring singly as contra-distinguished from one of a pair". For much of my life I have lived unwedded or not as part of a pair or, in the language of the day, not partnered. It has not particularly worried me but it has been on occasions the subject of curiosity by others. As I have noted in ***Things Peripatetic***, when travelling as a single female much curiosity is directed towards the lack of a partner, particularly in America. When I turned up at a ball unaccompanied in 2013, I was asked where my partner was. When I responded that he had died 17 years ago, I was asked: "Why have you not remarried?". How do you respond to a question like that? I think that I responded rather facetiously that he was too good an act to follow and left the matter there. I have now lived unpartnered for over 20 years and find that I am content with my lot and my space. There is so much that one can do alone with personal satisfaction and pleasure and much that can be done with company but being "partnered" is not an essential ingredient of any of it. I have many male friends who do not and are not inclined to make inroads into my accepted lifestyle. I am not lonely. I have the absolute freedom to choose company and conversations: my time and inclinations are my own: I am content with my lot. I have plenty of **things still to be done**.

My wonderful *Lloyd's Encyclopaedic Dictionary* defines "mellow" in a number of ways but I would rather like to think that listed meaning No 5 might be appropriate to where I am now in body and soul: well matured; ripened or softened by years; jovial; good-humoured, hearty.

Well matured; ripened or softened by years; jovial; good-humoured, hearty.
Enjoying a mother and son moment of humour.

11. Things Not Done

Things Not Done — Not at all — Not by choice — For want of skill

The recent acquisition of a sister-in-law in the early 1960s drew my attention to the fact that there were things that I could not do or had not learnt how to do. For her it was an achievement that she could do something that I could not do and no doubt this elevated her self-esteem in some way. The act of drawing to my attention the fact that there were things that one couldn't do or didn't have the enthusiasm to do or the skill to do has become very informative in relation to the presentation of this memoir. So here are a few of the things which I have not done or not done at all or not had the skill to do.

Playing cards

For some unknown reason I have always had difficulty in following complicated card games. As children we played many simple card games but in later years when my brothers were experts in things like poker and a very fast game called *up and down the river*, I either did not have the inclination or will to be interested in pursuing the matter. I still find it very difficult to become involved in a complex card game. In later years people have suggested that it might be time to take up Bridge. I'm afraid I have not yet acquired the enthusiasm to do so. Nonetheless I did enjoy Mahjong for several years.

Singing

In retrospect I suspect I was tone-deaf. I grasped a fairly decent knowledge of the theory of music in primary school. No one ever told me not to sing and I participated as frequently as possible. From an early age I enjoyed singing hymns and I suspect that that was because nobody ever asked me not to sing. At secondary school, I sang in House choirs and in morning assembly, without being admonished. It was only when my young son, wearing the badge of honour of the Shore Junior School choir at a public church service, poked me in the ribs and told me in no uncertain terms "don't sing" that I took a step back.

Music

I regret so much that I do not have a memory for music. I can hear something and enjoy listening but, if I hear it tomorrow or next week, I do not recognise it as something I have heard before. I once took myself off to a U3A course on appreciating classical music. I was rather hoping that it might help me to remember some of the music that I heard playing a lot of the time. It did not happen but I did come more to grips with what I was hearing. I was introduced to Chamber Music in Trinity College, Cambridge, one evening when on a Summer School there and came away enamoured. I still enjoy small ensembles far more than anything else and do on occasions remember something I have heard before. I suspect it is the small number of players and instruments.

Dancing

Anecdotes that I recall relate to a maypole event in primary school which was really just a lot of skipping rather than dancing. In late teens we would go dancing at the fortnightly dance in a hall at Thornlands. When fully dressed and ready to go out my brother would remind me of the steps of the dances that might be on the program. Those lessons, in great haste as we were about to leave home, must have stood me in quite good stead because I did manage to be able to follow the music and dance in all later years. I may not have been a good dancer but I wasn't an embarrassment as far as I recall.

Book clubbing

I seem never to have had time or opportunity to join a book club and think that the time may have passed me by. I am still an avid, prolific and eclectic reader. I spend time with friends talking about books we are reading and passing on new titles.

The very state of being alive must mean that there are still things to do and with the pace of change in this inventive, innovative world there will always be things not done. So be it.

Epilogue

Today I sat and thought
And wondered why and how and when
The failings with which life is fraught
Are well beyond my ken.
On and on we go from day to day
To what and how and when?
We work to acquire to use to pay
To be able to say we are men
Why for? Wherefore? And when?

There must in life be something,
A reward for all that is done,
An end to the heights, the levels and sinking,
To some so petty, so large for some.
What is to be looked for tomorrow
When all of today's labour is done?
Repetition of today's trial and error.
Will it, should it ever be gone
Today, tomorrow and done?

Index

About the Author

Naida Haxton was born in Brisbane and grew up at Cleveland during the 1940s and 1950s. She was educated at Cleveland State Primary School and Somerville House in Brisbane, completed degrees in Arts and Law at the University of Queensland, was admitted to practice as a barrister in 1966 (the first woman to actively practise at the Queensland Bar) and almost immediately began receiving briefs. Her practice was, to begin with, "commercial work, probate work, bankruptcy and some family law".

In 1967 she received her first junior brief in the Supreme Court and in 1969, her first brief in the High Court. She also lectured at the University of Queensland in Land Law and Commercial Law, and frequently made speeches to women's organisations and other bodies.

She moved after marriage to Sydney and was admitted to the NSW Bar in early 1972 and remained in practice until 2006.

From 1972 to 1981, Naida was Editor of the Papua New Guinea Law Reports.

In 1981, she was appointed Assistant Editor of the NSW Law Reports until 2000 when she became the Editor. As Editor of authorised law reports she was proactive in converting paper reports to electronic formats. Naida also lectured at the University of Sydney and the University of Technology Sydney and for the NSW Bar Association continuing education program.

Naida was involved in many community activities including as Director, Deputy Chair and Chair of the Board Advisory Committee for BoysTown in Brisbane between 2004 and 2014.

She was conferred an Order of Australia in 2007 for her services to the legal profession and to the judiciary, particularly as Editor of the NSWLR and as a practitioner and educator.

Haxton Chambers in Brisbane is named in Naida's honour.

Relevant publications

Naida J Haxton: A Manual on Law Reporting 1991 published with assistance from The Federation Press and funding from the Law Foundation of New South Wales and republished in 2003.

N J Haxton: Law Reporting and Risk Management - Citing Unreported Judgments 2001, 185 ABR 84.

J M Bennett and N J Haxton: Law Reporting and Legal Authoring, *No Mere Mouthpiece, Servants of All — Yet of None*, LexisNexis Butterworths, Australia, 2002, 145.

Naida Haxton: Law Reporting: Rebutting some Assumptions: Law Book Co (2006) 80 ALJR 341

NJ Haxton: Editing judgments: lessons learned in the world of law reporting: Clarity (Journal of the international association promoting plain legal language) (2007) No 57 at 28.